Making Children's Costumes

MAKING CHILDREN'S COSTUMES

by

Priscilla Lobley

TAPLINGER PUBLISHING COMPANY
NEW YORK

First published in the United States in 1972 by
TAPLINGER PUBLISHING CO., INC.
New York, New York

Library of Congress Catalog Card Number: 77-185256
ISBN 0-8008-5077-7

*The author would like to acknowledge
the invaluable help of Robert and
Benjamin Lobley*

Contents

1 INTRODUCTION   *page* 13

2 STARTING THE PROJECT   16

3 SIMPLE DRESSMAKING   21

4 THE PHOTOGRAPHS EXPLAINED   26
    Marmalade Cat   26
    Butterfly   29
    Spanish Gypsy   33
    Witch   36
    Milkmaid   39
    Nurse   42
    Mediaeval Princess   44
    Crusader   48
    Indo-Persian Warrior   54
    Roman Soldier   59
    Cowboy   62
    Red Indian Chieftain   65
    Spaceman   67
    Robot No. 163007,445921   70

5 PARTIES   73
    Policeman   73
    Little Red Riding Hood   74
    Pirate   75
    Hawaiian Girl   76
    Surgeon   77
    Harebell   78
    Roman Citizen   79
    Little Bo-Peep   80
    Chinese Mandarin   81

CONTENTS

Egyptian Lady   *page* 82
Arab   83
Harem Girl   84
Jester   85
Mouse   86
King   86
Queen   87
Harlequin   88
Columbine   89
Clown   90
A few crazy ideas   91

6 MASKS AND MAKE-UP   92

Plates

I. Marmalade Cat and Butterfly   *page* 30

II. Spanish Gypsy and Witch   35

III. Milkmaid and Nurse   41

IV. Mediaeval Princess   45

V. Crusader   51

VI. Indo-Persian Warrior and Roman Soldier   58

VII. Cowboy and Red Indian Chieftain   64

VIII. Spaceman and Robot   71

Photographs by Peter Marston

Glossary

broderie Anglaise—edging ribbon with open embroidery
Copydex—fabric glue
Evo-Stik—a very strong impact glue (use Elmer's or Sobo)
Fablon—contact paper
ironmongers—hardware store
nappy pin—diaper or safety pin
off-cuts—remnants
plimsolls—light canvas shoes with rubber soles, as sneakers
Polyfilla—modeling paste, as gesso
petersham—buckram
sempstress—seamstress
Staflex—iron-on pellon
Stanley knife—a short-bladed utility knife for cutting cardboard or linoleum
Vilene—interfacing, similar to pellon
Weetabix packet—cereal carton
Wellingtons—rubber boots

CHAPTER 1

Introduction

The excitement of dressing up starts very early in life and one never quite grows out of it. Children are constantly thrilled by creating their own fantasies with clothes, and the outfits you make for them will never lie idle in a drawer. It is a vital part in the development of a child's awareness and self-confidence and to make-believe is fun for anyone from time to time.

I think you can divide dressing-up clothes into three main categories. Firstly, ones that supply a basic need like wanting to grow up, amuse friends, and frighten foes. There need be no reality in this sort. A little girl will happily stomp around in her mother's outsize shoes. A large paper sack with head painted on will serve quite satisfactorily as a lion and a sleeping-bag will turn even a timid child into a monster. Secondly, there are the clothes you get together for a fancy dress party, which is very much a worn-once-only occasion. When making these outfits, skilful adaptation of existing clothes should be made whenever possible. As 12 p.m. strikes and the coach turns back to a pumpkin it can be disconcerting to lose the policeman's jacket to a school blazer, and the Arab's robes or Roman toga back to the bed-clothes, but this is the fun of creating a complete, if superficial, illusion and the clothes survive to take another part some other time. Thirdly, there are the costumes that you make as authentically as possible, but also with the minimum of expense. In order to relate them with reasonable accuracy to what they are supposed to portray, you have to find out what they are meant to look like. One learns something new all the time! I have found out, amongst other things, for instance, that real Red Indian trousers were made from antelope skin and did not cover the bottom, and that Crusaders' linen surcoats were worn to keep the sun off the chain mail: interesting facts that will not necessarily help you with your dressmaking. These outfits should be made to be worn again and again as they will form the basis for the children's dressing-up ritual. You will also probably be asked from time to time to make them for school plays.

The difficult job is to make things tough and long-lasting enough. Boys especially are not prone to respecting handiwork and if engaged in battle games, they really have not much time for it. Girls are usually more ladylike in their pursuits but are still given to destructive habits. So, if clothes are to be worn just once to a party the emphasis can simply be on effect. Otherwise things should be made really strong.

Cost, too, is an important factor, and obviously the less spent the better. Jumble sales can be a fruitful source for old hats, curtains, sheets, even interesting clothes if you can face the jostle. Take a look at the fabric stalls in your local market for materials, ribbons, zips, etc. The bargains to be found are amazing. Remnants from department stores can also be bought as an economy. Try to start collecting supplies for a dressing-up drawer, because children prefer dressing up with their friends and you can never have too many potential outfits. If you do not possess a spare drawer for keeping things together you may find that large egg-box cartons from your local supermarket will answer the purpose. You could use one for clothes and another for props like hats, helmets, swords, handbags, and cover the boxes with wallpaper or Fablon to strengthen them and improve their appearance.

The pleasing thing about making fancy dress is the amount of co-operation and help one receives from all participants. Everyone seems to want to join in. Little ones can only help by their enthusiasm but older children can be useful assistants in all sorts of ways. They are often very good at finding out about things from books and museums, and can develop a real taste for research. Of course one cannot over-emphasize the fact that finding out what clothes people used to wear makes history more alive and interesting to a child.

A visit to the Tower of London, if at all possible, is invaluable if you are intent on making some armour. You have so much more visual knowledge to help you once you have seen the real thing, and the thrill of creating something that looks even a little like it, gives one tremendous satisfaction. When I was first asked for a cowboy outfit I was keen to make something entirely different from the usual run of 'the plastic Roy Rogers sort'. I was certain that real cowboys' clothes never looked quite like these, having visited the American museum in Claverton (though, of course, you have to be in the West Country to do this). In this delightful museum they are very much concerned with displaying the U.S.A. as it really was in the days of the early settlers. Here, in their Wild West display, there is the smell of real leather, and an atmosphere of the open plains and wandering herdsmen which is most evocative. With the real gear to look at, one certainly has a good basis to work from. One does not always have time or opportunity to see things in museums or art galleries, but when one can it is certainly well worth it. Information from books is much more easily acquired and most public libraries will be helpful in assisting you to find the right book.

Making fancy dress is also a useful way to introduce kids to a bit of dressmaking. After all, the standard does not have to be too high and some simple machining could well be left to an elder girl or boy. Cutting out cardboard can be a little tricky and dangerous but simple papier mâché can be done by most children if you keep an eye on them. They can also co-operate on any painting jobs to be done. Patterns on Red Indian clothes, for example, emblems on shields, patterns on wings, faces on animal heads, and they are very handy with silver paint sprays. There are also things to be cut out, and stuck down in place. Jewels that are made out of shiny glitter paper, and patterns that are cut from felt fabric and paper.

Children should be encouraged by every means to develop their innate sense of self-expression. Although they love playing for its own sake and without any effort will invent their own imaginative games, they also like the enterprise and discipline of organized play-acting and drama.

Christmas or school holidays can suddenly become times for the thrilling activities of writing plays, dressing up actors, moving round furniture and putting on the grand entertainment.

CHAPTER 2

Starting the Project

It would be impossible to describe how to make every character, real or imaginary, that a child might wish to be, but I have tried to make the instructions for the fourteen outfits in Chapter 4 as clear and detailed as possible, so that once you have made a few of these outfits you will probably be able to go on to ideas of your own. The aim of this chapter is to describe in general terms some useful techniques that will help you make fancy dress more easily, and to expand a bit on how and where to obtain the various materials.

The first decision to be made is 'what to be?' and I hope that some of the ideas in this book will do to start you off. The stumbling block to making anything is often a lack of imagination and visual memory. Once you know in your mind what something should look like, then the hard part is over. Reference to books is the quickest way of finding what one wants to know. If the right one is not on your own bookshelf, take a trip to your local library where you are bound to find something that will be helpful.

The history of clothes and fashion is a fascinating subject and there have been many good books written about it. Authorities such as James Laver and Phillis Cunnington have provided many, and the latter's *Costume in Pictures* which is in an inexpensive paperback edition, is a particularly beautiful combination of art and fashion. I also recommend Margot Lister's excellent illustrated survey, which covers a vast range of costumes and shows them with clear easy-to-follow drawings, making it an ideal book for the stage designer and the fancy-dress maker. Other library sections that are worth looking at for reference are Art, History and Stage-Craft, and children's books often have illustrations that are accurate and informative. Having decided what you are going to make, here are some tips on materials before you make a start.

FABRICS

Ordinary worn-out cotton sheets make an excellent all-purpose material, in the cheapest possible way. There are no seams to unpick and garments can be made with as few joins as possible. The cotton absorbs dye economically and well, so long as you remember to keep stirring it all the time, and can be completely transformed with colour and decoration. If you buy material by the yard look out for fabrics that do not fray too easily because you want to avoid the extra work of finishing edges. Upholstery materials often let you down badly in this way. For exotic and glittering fabrics try cheap market stalls where there is often a wider selection than in many department stores. Felt can be bought in squares of various colours from shop needlework departments and is useful for such things as heraldic motifs, animal noses, waistcoats, etc. Net (tulle) for fairies' or ballet dancers' dresses is nowadays made out of nylon so is extremely strong and uncrushable. However, do not press it with a hot iron as you will simply be left with a hole.

LEATHER

This is something one always seems to need, whether it is for belts or scabbards, chaps or straps. I must admit to having years ago discarded a worn-out suede coat which I firstly made into a child's jacket, and then into innumerable belts and re-inforcements for other worn-out garments. Its final bits have been made into invaluable assets for our family dressing-up collection. I am not suggesting that everyone has a similar old coat lying around to be cut up, but if you ever have a chance of getting one, do not let it go. Imitation leather is a very convincing alternative and can be bought by the yard in stores and do-it-yourself shops. American cloth and Vinyl are two good examples. The latter is used in car upholstery and is available in many leather patterns and colours. The only drawback to it can be the thickness of the plastic coating which sometimes makes it difficult to stick. American cloth which is lighter and more flexible is easier to fix in place. Sometimes you can buy these materials in street-market stalls where they are sold as off-cuts.

CARDBOARD

You can take away free from your supermarket practically any size or shape of box, and the packaging revolution has certainly given fresh scope to those with ideas for making things. What you need to look out for is the difference in the types of board used to make up the boxes, which is usually either corrugated board (crinkled card sandwiched between two layers) or cardboard (card glued solid and compressed). By far the most suitable is the latter but it is not the type most commonly used in cartons. For cutting and moulding it holds its shape with more rigidity than the corrugated board, which although thicker and stronger has a tendency to crease easily along its ridges, making it unsuitable for headgear, swords and armour. If you stick two or three layers of cardboard together and cut them out for a sword, you will have something amazingly strong but flexible. If you do the same with corrugated board, the thing bends in half the first time that it is thrust into an opponent's body, which means a lot of wasted effort.

TOOLS FOR CUTTING

Cardboard is a very tough material to cut and unless you have the correct tools to handle it, you will probably give up in despair. I should definitely invest in a Stanley knife or a similar type of craft tool, and a steel or steel-edged ruler. As these knives are exceedingly strong and sharp, the business of cutting the card up becomes a satisfying and easy job. I must insert a warning against carelessness. Always concentrate on what you are doing, and never leave the knife where it could be picked up by a young child. In order to cut boxes up they must first be flattened and all staples removed. I do my cutting on the floor, but you must have a thick layer of corrugated board already down to cut out on, otherwise you will find yourself slicing up the lino. Hold your ruler firmly down where you wish to cut and take the knife down as close to it as possible (Fig. 1). Two or three cuts will be sufficient to slice right

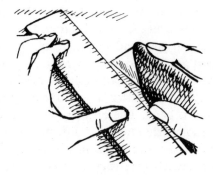

FIG. 1

through the cardboard. Light card such as is made into cereal packs also has its uses and this can be cut up with scissors. If possible have a large pair which can be kept exclusively for paper and card cutting because this so quickly blunts the blades.

Another item which is invaluable for quickly securing cardboard together is a stapler—those gadgets that put permanent metal tacks in things. They are not too expensive to buy and can be very handy to have around the house for other jobs as well.

GLUES

There is a wide choice in handicraft shops and stationers, and in case you are not sure what glue to use for a particular job I list below my own preferences.

1. *P.V.A.* (Polyvinyl Acetate emulsion)   A relatively new type of glue which is indispensable in any household. It sticks most things quickly and effectively. Although it appears white in the tube, it dries absolutely transparent, which makes it ideal for sticking paper and fabric. It is also extremely strong and will satisfactorily join cardboard and even wood. It can be thinned down with water and used to make a very strong papier mâché but it is a little expensive to use in this way. Casco make one called Glue-all, and Gloy make one called Multiglue.

2. *Evo-Stik*   Use this glue when a tremendously strong bond is needed, for example, on joints of armour.

3. *Copydex*   Use this glue for fabrics and surfaces that need to be kept flexible. It will also seal edges of material.

4. *Polycell wallpaper paste*   This is one of the cheapest glues to use for papier mâché. You may not be too familiar with this useful process which can either be used to make a strong moulded shape for masks or give a smooth ready-to-paint finish to rough surfaces. First mix your glue in a shallow dish: then, using tissue paper if possible, tear paper up into small pieces. (Torn edges blend together much better than cut ones.) Submerge paper pieces in glue, and place as smoothly as possible over the required surface. Smooth out all wrinkles and cover as neatly and evenly as possible. Allow to dry until surface is rock hard.

TAPES FOR JOINING CARDBOARD

Masking tape (Sellotape X) which you can buy from most stationers is a stretchy self-adhesive tape which is excellent for joining edges of cardboard together. Its great advantage is that it holds a join instantly, but it is expensive to use in any quantity. Much cheaper, and as satisfactory in most ways, is brown sticky paper, which is also bought on rolls from stationers. You can buy it in 1-inch and 2-inch widths and although it has to be held in place for a minute or two whilst it dries it is very good stuff to use.

VELCRO

This is a marvellous invention. Two tapes of tiny hooks and loops hold fast together, adopting the same principle as the burr, and making a remarkably strong way of joining two edges temporarily together. Indispensable for back seams, belts, etc.

MISCELLANEOUS

Haberdashery departments have a wide selection of decorative upholstery and lamp-shade binding edgings and these are useful for adding embellishment to many things. When wire is needed to add strength to wings, etc., buy galvanized wire from the ironmongers. You buy it in 1 lb. coils in various thicknesses from 20 gauge (thin) to 9 gauge (thick); 16–18 gauge are good standard sizes to have. If you need a more delicate wire for a very small fairy or perhaps certain head-dresses buy a small coil of white millinery (cotton covered) wire from a haberdashery department.

For painting card and fabric use poster paints, which are water soluble and are therefore easier for children to handle. Unfortunately they will not be permanent and so you will not be able to wash the fabric. Simple repeating patterns can be printed on material by using potato or swede cuts. Slice the vegetable in half, mark pattern required, and cut away surplus with a pointed kitchen knife so that you have a raised shape to print with. Mix colour fairly thick with a little wallpaper paste to bind it. If you feel more ambitious and have already done some lino cutting you can print your designs from this using an oil-based fabric ink, which will have the advantage of being quite washable.

When silver, gold or copper is needed use paint sprays from Woolworth's, for though expensive to buy, they last a long time, and will save you money on brushes and turpentine.

CHAPTER 3

Simple Dressmaking

You don't need any dressmaking skill to make the sort of garments that are wanted for most fancy dress outfits. Clothes will last longer if they do not fit (i.e. are made too big) and the standard of sewing should not aim at perfection. If one looks at the clothes of many earlier civilizations you will find they often consisted of a simple rectangle of cloth that sometimes had no stitching at all. It could be worn as a cloak, which was fastened on the shoulder, or wrapped round waist and hips as a kilt, or draped round the body sari and toga fashion, or sometimes sewn together down one side and kept in place with leather girdles. Indian, Arab, Greek and Roman clothes are all based on the use of draped cloth so these make good outfits for the lazy sempstress. Figs. 2, 3, 4 and 5 show ways of wrapping cloaks, kilts and togas.

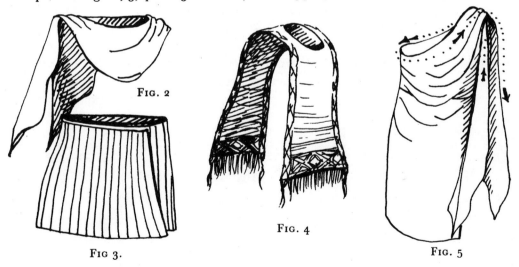

FIG. 2

FIG 3.

FIG. 4

FIG. 5

The Greeks devised a garment called the Chiton which was also adopted and worn by the Romans. Made from a rectangle of material, it was folded in half and the two short sides were stitched together. The Greeks joined one of the longer sides with brooches to form the shoulder seams, but for a child to wear they are better gathered

21

up and stitched leaving a large opening in the middle for the head and smaller ones each end for the arms (Fig. 6). It can be allowed to fall to the ground as a simple dress or gathered up in folds with a girdle round the chest, waist and hips (see Fig. 7). A simple variation was the Doric Chiton which used a wider rectangle of material folded over so that the extra width formed a decorative layer (Fig. 8). The next progression from unstitched draperies was the T-shaped tunic. This garment is still

FIG. 6

FIG. 7

FIG. 8

a most simple and economical way of covering the human body, and it can be used as the foundation dress for many different outfits. You cut it out all in one piece with an opening for the head made in the centre (see Fig. 9). The only sewing that has to be done is down the two side seams. If you wish to add long sleeves, cut off short sleeve on pattern where shown (Fig. 10). Cut sleeves desired length. Join to tunic at shoulder line, and then sew down length of sleeve and side of tunic all in one opera-

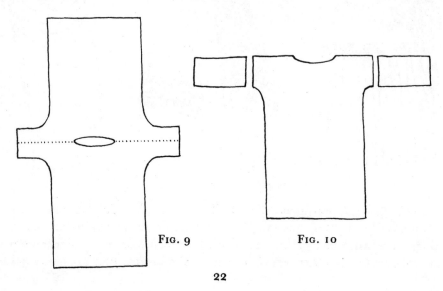

FIG. 9

FIG. 10

tion. Although the T-shaped tunic is a very adaptable garment some dresses for girls obviously require a closer fit and it is helpful therefore to know how to cut a simple bodice. First measure the child, referring when necessary to Fig. 11, making sure the tape is neither too loose nor too tight.

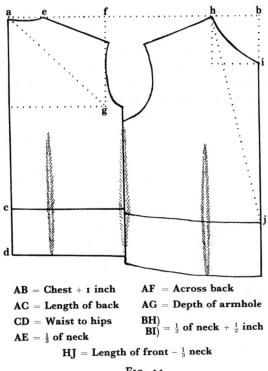

AB = Chest + 1 inch   AF = Across back
AC = Length of back   AG = Depth of armhole
CD = Waist to hips   BH) BI) = ⅓ of neck + ½ inch
AE = ⅓ of neck

HJ = Length of front − ⅓ neck

FIG. 11

1. *Round chest* Take tape round largest part making sure it is level all round.
2. *Round waist*
3. *Round neck*
4. *Length front* Take tape measure from centre back of neck letting it follow round natural contour of neck and diagonally down chest to centre of waist-line. From this deduct one-third of neck measurement.
5. *Length back*
6. *Across back*
7. *Depth of armhole* This is taken by placing a ruler high under armpit (keep it horizontal) and measure from the centre of neck to the end of ruler. Make a drawing from diagram as shown, drawing in armholes and shoulder lines as shown and placing darts in centre of each section. Take in side edges slightly at waist. Make ½ inch (1·5 cm.) seam allowance all the way round and cut out ready for use. If this all seems like too much trouble and you want a short cut put some paper down on the table,

lay on it a dress that correctly fits the girl you are making the dress for, and draw round it with a pencil as close to the seams as possible. This done, re-draw so that the contours are similar to the fitted bodice and draw in darts and seam allowance. Cut out. It will not be so accurate but you will probably do it a lot quicker, and if you are in a hurry this counts.

For simplification, skirts for children can be divided into two categories: those that are cut flared and those that are cut straight.

The straight variety are often gathered at the waist, so that there is sufficient room around the hemline for the wearer to move, i.e. the dirndl skirt. It is more economical in material and is flattering to small slim children. A very easily made dirndl skirt that will never be outgrown can be made without side seams like an elongated apron (see Fig. 12). Cut a very long length of material, gather it up as much as possible and

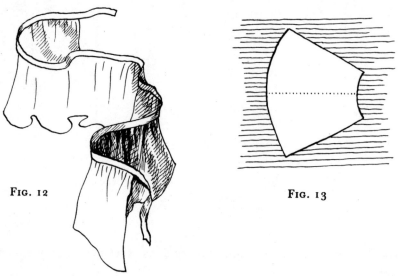

FIG. 12   FIG. 13

stitch on to a strip of material approx. 4 inches × 4 feet (10 cm. × 1·2 m.). This can then be wound round a child's waist two to three times, allowing her to grow as fast as she likes. A particularly good way of doing this skirt is with the top of a sheet so that the machine edging forms a very pretty hemline—see Milkmaid's outfit, page 41.

The advantage of the flared skirt is that it hangs nice and full without any surplus material on the waist and hips—see Mediaeval Princess outfit, page 44. It can be made any size from two quarters of a circle to two halves of a circle. The centres back and front of a skirt are always placed on the straight of the material parallel to the selvedge edges (see Fig. 13) and when you are putting up hems remember that sewing stitches should be very, very loose.

Another basic garment that you will need to know how to cut is trousers. Like the bodice you can always cut a pattern from a pair of existing ones, especially as it is wise to cut them generously large. If you would prefer to cut a pattern see Fig. 14. Take waist and inside leg measurement. Note that centre back is considerably longer than the front and cut more on the bias to allow extra room for sitting down. To turn trousers into an all-in-one suit simply place bodice pattern on top, waist to waist, and cut out together. Now that tights are popular wear for children of all ages, they are often the most suitable way of covering the legs in outfits for many periods of costume.

Here are a few final points. Try and persuade children to dress for a party in outfits particularly suited to them. A plump girl will make a more attractive Red Riding Hood than a fairy. A skinny boy will make a good Jack Sprat and a large boy a splendid King and so on.

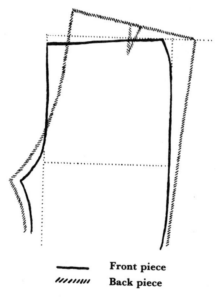

—————— Front piece
//////// Back piece

FIG. 14

Keep up to date with your children when dealing with contemporary figures. The most important things for a child—and what they enjoy most—are the details, which they will probably know more about than you, and they will want the very latest points to be featured. Fancy dress is often inclined to be uncomfortable to wear so make sure it is as easy as possible for the child to get on and off. Wherever possible make use of Velcro, elastic and zips, and make sure head openings are plenty large enough. It is a pity for clothes to be needlessly torn and ruined the first time they are worn, because certain difficulties had not been anticipated.

25

CHAPTER 4

The Photographs Explained

The outfits in this chapter are all illustrated in the photographs, and none are particularly difficult to make, though most have had some care taken in the sewing to ensure that they stand up to wear and tear. Some of the materials needed involve a certain amount of expense, but this can be kept to a minimum and some (like the Robot) need cost nothing at all.

N.B. Do not forget to add $\frac{1}{2}$ inch (1·5 cm.) seam allowances on all the patterns that you make.

MARMALADE CAT
(Plate I)

Strictly speaking this is an all-purpose animal outfit that can be adapted to become a mouse, a rabbit or a hare. If you come by any woolly or furry material, like fur fabric, this will obviously be ideal, but these fabrics can be very expensive to buy, especially as one uses a large quantity of material. I have used a shiny orange furnishing fabric with a texture of hair-like lines, which gives an effect of a silky marmalade cat when painted all over with stripes.

For jump suit: Depends a great deal on the size of child, but approx. 3 yards (2·7 m.) of suitable material. Black felt for nose and paws

For head: $\frac{3}{8}$ yard (34·5 cm.) of very stiff buckram. Bristles from a broom for whiskers. Poster paint

For tail: Kapok or hay

Jump suit Cut a pattern from a pair of long trousers adding 1 inch (2·5 cm.) all round for extra width, but taking 2 inches (5 cm.) off at natural waist line. Extend trousers at ankles so that front part goes over foot and back part covers ankles. Cut a pattern for top part from an old jersey, adding extra at neckline in order to cover neck. Finish at 3 inches (7·5 cm.) below natural waist line, cut sleeves remembering to extend and join ends to make into paws (see Fig. 15). Join up all seams, put a facing on neckline and if possible sew a zip down centre back for an opening. (This may present difficulties for a young child to get in and out of, in which case put a zip or strip of Velcro down centre front.) Cut out felt paws—4 toes and 1 pad for each hand (Fig. 16). Stick on inside of sleeve. Make your tail from a strip about 20 inches (51 cm) long and 8 inches (23 cm.) wide. Sew it into a long sausage with a pointed end. Turn inside out and fill up with kapok or hay. Paint on stripes with wild abandon: use brown first and darken still further with crimson and black. Lastly, sew on tail.

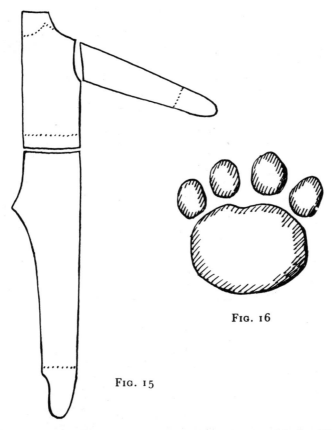

FIG. 16

FIG. 15

Head The pattern given would fit a child up to 12 years old. See Fig. 17, and make sure your drawing on either graph paper or your own measured one-inch squares. If you like you can make a pattern in light card first, and fit on child's head to check size and fit. Cut out shape in buckram. The reason I use this material is that it is stronger and more pliable than ordinary cardboard, and it is easier to sew. Cut out exactly the same shape in your 'cat' material, plus two ears in double thickness. See Fig. 18 for shape. Stick material to buckram with Copydex or P.V.A. glue. (A worthwhile extra at this stage would be to line inside of buckram with soft paper or

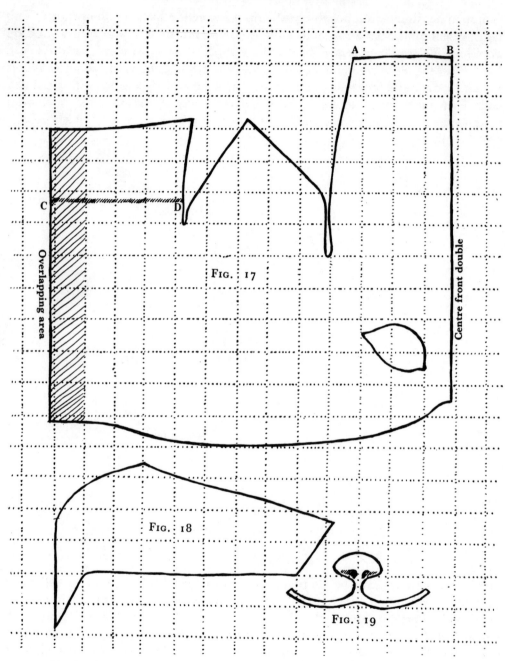

Overlapping area

C   D

FIG. 17

A   B

Centre front double

FIG. 18

FIG. 19

Each square measures 1 inch by 1 inch (2.5cm)

thin material. This would prevent the natural roughness of buckram scratching the wearer's face.) Sew ears round top edge and turn inside out. Cut holes for eyes and apply more glue if necessary. Join the overlapping area that is shown in the diagram by shading and sew securely together. Take AB across to CD to form head and sew in place. Put ears on as shown in photograph, Plate I, inserting the buckram ear piece in the middle of the two layers. Cut out a nose in felt (see Fig. 19) and sew in place. Paint stripes all over in the same way as the jump suit, and paint the nose pink except for the nostrils. Finally sew a few bristles in place above eyes as well as for whiskers. Fig. 20 shows you how by altering the shape and placing of the eyes, nose and ears, this head may be easily made into other animals.

FIG. 20

BUTTERFLY
(Plate I)

Choose a colour scheme and stick to it throughout. The one illustrated is in magenta, orange and copper. An all-white outfit would also make a pretty 'Cabbage White' butterfly if you painted the patterns on the wings a greenish-black.

For dress: 2 yards (1·8 m.) of magenta net (48 inches wide); ⅜ yard (34·5 cm.) of some
    sort of shimmery matching material; 5 buttons about ¾ inch (2 cm.) in diameter
For wings: 1 yard (90 cm.) of white tailoring canvas; 20 gauge galvanized wire and
    white bias binding
Extras: Orange or tan coloured tights; copper metallic paint spray for wings

Dress Divide the net into three long strips each 16 inches (40·5 cm.) wide. Do not worry about the centre crease. It will not show if you place it underneath the two other layers. If you would like to press it out, remember to use a very cool iron, otherwise it will disappear into holes. Cut a fitted bodice out of the shimmery material with two darts in the front and two at the back. In the front of the bodice cut a V-

I. MARMALADE CAT AND BUTTERFLY

shaped neckline about 4 to 5 inches (10 to 12·5 cm.) deep. Leave the neck set high at the back in order that five strong buttonholes and buttons may be sewn down the centre back. When you make the wings you will sew four large buttonholes in the centre, which will fasten up to the bottom four buttons on the dress. This will be an easy, safe and effective way of keeping the wings in place. I advise you to put some strengthening material underneath the buttons and buttonholes on the dress to give a little extra support (see Fig. 21). For the sleeves cut a puff sleeve pattern in net measuring about 19½ inches (50 cm.) in width and 4½ inches (11·5 cm.) in length (see Fig. 22).

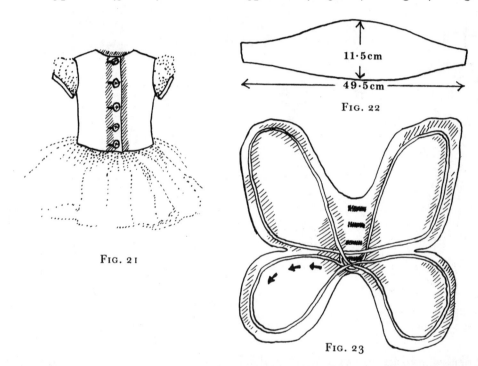

FIG. 21

11·5 cm

49·5 cm

FIG. 22

FIG. 23

From the bodice fabric cut two short lengths (to fit round arms) about 1½ inches (4 cm.) wide. Having seamed the sleeves, gather them up as much as possible at bottom so that they fit with the edging strips. Sew them together, then gather edge up at top of sleeve and sew into bodice. When sewing skirt lengths of net to dress, do not seam together. Simply gather each one up as much as possible and sew round one after the other. Fit on child and measure desired length of net. Lay dress on a table and cut along hemline in neat 4-inch (10 cm.) V's. An addition of a small frill round neckline looks quite fetching.

Wings Ask how big the wearer wants her wings to be. It is important for her to feel the size is just right. I was requested by a very small girl for very large wings and the size I have given may be the size that others would like too. First look at Fig. 23 or

31

check in a book to see what shape butterflies' wings are, and draw a similar shape on the canvas 32 inches (81·5 cm.) at widest point and 26 inches (66 cm.) at highest point. Cut out. Uncoil a 15-foot (4·5 m.) length of 20 gauge galvanized wire and curve it round wings in the shape drawn in diagram. Using a liberal coating of P.V.A. glue stick wire in place and then stick the bias binding on top of it as a covering. (If you wish to make very light fairy-like wings in organza, you should use

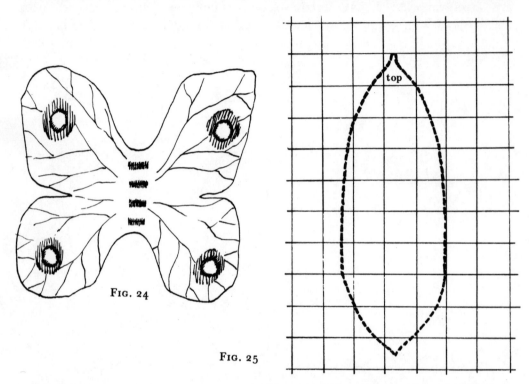

FIG. 24

FIG. 25

millinery wire to achieve a really ethereal effect.) The next job is painting and for this I should use poster paints or similar water-based colour. First draw in the main lines of pattern with a blue-black colour. Don't worry if the effect looks too strong. The harshness will be softened later on. Next splash on lots of watery colour in blue and green, to give the iridescence of butterfly wings, and to strengthen the pattern. Leave paint to dry absolutely. Spray all over lightly with copper paint. Finally cut four large circles in orange material and four smaller ones in the magenta dress material. Stick on to wings as shown in Fig. 24 with Copydex or P.V.A. glue. Make four button-holes in centre 1¼ inches (3 cm.) in length to join to dress.

Cap Cut out six pieces as in Fig. 25 adding a ¼-inch (6 mm.) seam allowance round dotted line. Each square on the pattern represents 1 inch (2·5 cm.). Sew them to-gether, and turn cap inside out. Spray all over with copper paint.

SPANISH GYPSY
(Plate II)

This is a pretty dress for a girl who likes dancing.

For dress: About 4¾ yards (4·3 cm.) of bright cotton fabric. This sounds a lot but unless
    the skirt is very full you will not achieve an authentic effect; 7½ yards (6·9 m.) of
    braid, the cheapest you can buy, such as ric-rac
For mantilla: ½ yard (45 cm.) of lace or near substitute
For camellia: Small piece of crêpe paper (pink, white or red) and some millinery wire
Extras: A Spanish fan

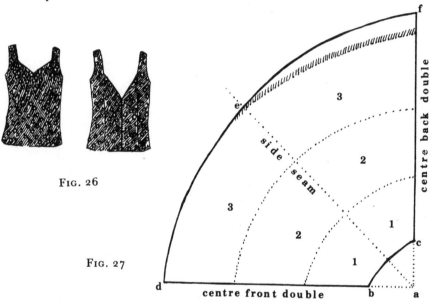

FIG. 26

FIG. 27

Dress Make or adapt a pattern for the bodice that fits into the waist and finishes
on hip-line. (Small children, about 3 inches (7·5 cm.) below waist, and bigger
children 4 inches (10 cm.).) It should have two darts in the front and back, and the
neckline cut away as indicated in Fig. 26. To make patterns for the skirt frills proceed as follows (see Fig. 27). Measure child down centre front, from waist to ankles.
From this subtract her waist to hip measurement (already established for the bodice)
and this is your skirt length. On a large piece of paper, using the corner as a right
angle, draw a curve from B to C, which is half hip measurement plus 1 inch (2·5
cm.). From B measure D for skirt length which you have just taken. Draw a curve
round to E and F, increasing the measurement by 1 inch (2·5 cm.) at the side seam

33

and 3 inches (7·5 cm.) at the back. (This extra length at the back is a typical feature of these dresses.) Draw on frill curves as shown by dotted lines and mark them 'Frill 1 front', and 'Frill 1 back', etc. From this basic pattern you now have to make three rows of frills (in six pieces) and a skirt lining on which to stitch them down. The bottom frill is gathered and stitched on to the hem of the skirt lining, and the middle and top frills are gathered and stitched on to the centre and top edge of skirt lining.

To make pattern for lining Cut out round B, C, D, E and F and separate the back from the front by the side seam. Cut off bottom frills (Nos. 3) on both pieces and keep them carefully on one side. From the two pieces now left you cut your skirt lining. Either use your dress fabric or substitute a plain white cotton material. Remember to lay centre front and centre back on the fold of your fabric and allow ½ inch (1·5 cm.) all round for seams.

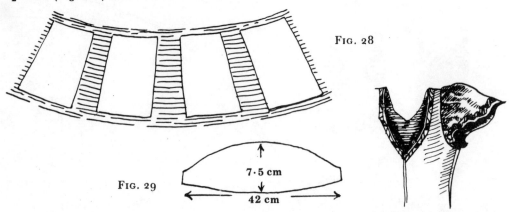

FIG. 28

FIG. 29

7·5 cm

42 cm

To make the frills The final job is to expand the basic frill patterns so that the pieces can be gathered up into full flounces. From your lining pattern separate frills Nos. 2 and Frills Nos. 1 in both pieces. Taking again the two bottom frills, Nos. 3, you now have six pieces. Cut each frill pattern into four pieces, being careful to maintain the curved shape, and spread out as shown in Fig. 28. Cut your six new patterns and re-label each of the frill pieces (e.g., Frill 2, Front). Place them on fabric, remembering to place centre front and centre back on the fold, and cut out.

Now cut up the rest of the material into bodice, frills, and sleeves (see Fig. 29). Assemble dress in usual way—darts first, side seams, shoulder seams. Oversew edges of sleeves and frills and then sew on braid. Gather up edges and attach frills to lining, bottom one first. Make sure that bodice fits well before you join it to skirt. Sew in sleeves, and a zip, if possible, down back of bodice.

Mantilla Make four pleats down one side of lace and sew down. Wear on top of head, keeping it fixed in place with hairpins.

34

II. SPANISH GYPSY AND WITCH

Gardenia Cut a small piece of crêpe paper 6 inches (15 cm.) long × 5 inches (12·5 cm.) wide. Cut five petals down each side as shown (Fig. 30). Be careful to see that the stretch of the paper goes across the petals. Screw up paper in centre. Cut a 4-inch (10 cm.) length of millinery wire and hook over centre of crêpe paper. Press wire very closely together with a pair of pliers, if you have them. Pull petals up, until they are all vertical and very close together. Shape the centre of each one by gently stretching the crêpe paper with the thumb and forefinger of each hand. Arrange petals so that they are equally spaced out. Paint a little green paint on wire and, if you like, for safety's sake, bend wire back double, so that there is no sharp edge to stick in anybody's eye.

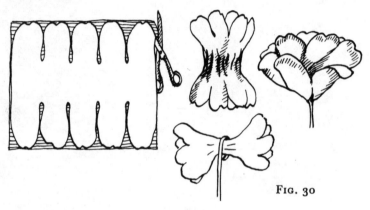

FIG. 30

WITCH
(Plate II)

The boys can wear this outfit as a wizard, but in this case you will not need jagged edges on the bottom of the cloak.

For hat: A sheet of light card or thick paper from a stationers or art shop to make cone.
Cardboard box to cut a square 12½ inches × 12½ inches (32 cm. × 32 cm.) for brim
For hair: String (sizal or polypropylene)
For cloak: 2 yards (1·8 m.) of any black material (48 inches (1·2 m.) wide). This will reach to the ankles of a 5-year-old and last until she is 12
For nose: A piece of card (the back of a cereal packet will do). A lump of Plasticine (any colour). P.V.A. glue or Polycell. Tissue paper—pink if possible (if you use any other colour you will also need some powder or poster paints). Shearing elastic
Extras: Borrow any old black clothes to wear underneath cloak. Black wellington boots. Birch besom

Hat Draw a shape on your card as shown in Fig. 31. The radius of the cone should measure 14 inches (35·5 cm.) and the overall shape should be just over a quarter of a circle. The area between A, B and C is where you start rolling round to form the cone and it will also help to strengthen the tip. Before you stick cone together place on the head of witch so that it fits snugly but not tightly. Staple or pin together and test again on head. Join seams inside and out with brown sticky paper (remove any pins). For the brim draw a circle from the bottom of the cone. If you press two sides together you will make an oval shape and this will fit the head more accurately. See Fig. 32. Draw brim about 2½ inches (6·5 cm.) wide round, and when you cut shape out, cut a fraction inside the circle for the crown in order for the cone to protrude slightly when the two are fitted together. Stick brim to crown with strong glue and when quite dry, paint over with black poster paint or ink.

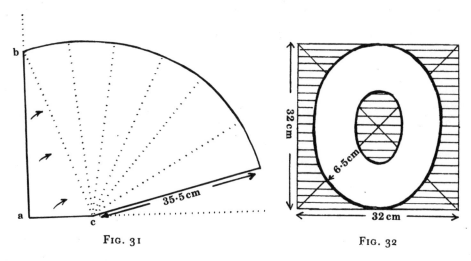

FIG. 31   FIG. 32

Hair Cut pieces of string to the required length, say 10 inches (25·5 cm) at back and 4 inches (10 cm.) at side, and unravel completely. Comb out so that it becomes fine like hair. Stick inside hat with Copydex by the following method. First lay out string on a formica surfaced table, in two lines of short strands for the sides, and two lines of long strands for the back. The string should be close together and the edge to be glued should be straight and tidy. Brush glue along these edges and round inside the brim. When both surfaces have become tacky, press them carefully together. Don't forget to leave a gap for the face!

Cloak Cut your rectangle of material into a semicircle as shown (Fig. 33) and cut a small curve 9 inches (23 cm.) wide and 4½ inches (11·5 cm.) deep in centre of selvedge edge to go round neck. Sew a strip of material about 1 yard (90 cm.) in length for cloak fastenings, and attach to neckline so you are left with two ties about 9 inches (23 cm.) long. Mark jagged edges round hem with tailor's chalk, and if you want to make a long-lasting garment, machine all along line with a close zig-zag stitch, and then cut round with sharp scissors. This will prevent any fraying. Cut out star and

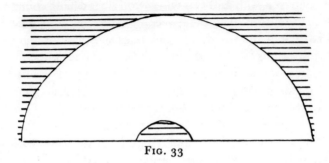

FIG. 33

moon shapes in fabric, felt or paper. Yellow, silver and blue are good mystical colours. Stick down with Copydex.

Nose   If you are using Polycell, first mix your glue. Stir a tablespoon into a 1-lb. jam jar of water, and allow to dissolve for $\frac{1}{4}$ hour, agitating it from time to time. Place a nose-sized lump of plasticine in the middle of the piece of card. Model the plasticine into the shape of a witch's nose, long and pointed as Fig. 34. Add hollow cheeks, smoothing out the plasticine on to the card so that is is quite thin round edges. When

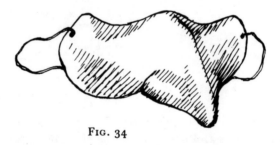

FIG. 34

you are satisfied with your nose, take your ready-mixed Polycell glue, or if you are using P.V.A. put some in a small bowl and thin it down a little with water. Tear up the tissue paper into small pieces, dip them well into glue, and smooth them on to the plasticine nose. Carry on smoothing out the tissue paper as you apply several layers. If you use small pieces of paper you will not have so many creases or air bubbles. When there is an even covering of tissue paper all over plasticine and spreading on to the card, leave everything to dry, preferably overnight. When it is rock hard, cut round edge of nose and cheeks with a sharp knife, and lift away from the card. It should be quite easy to pull plasticine out from inside the nose. Trim the edges neatly with scissors, and make two small holes at the sides to attach elastic. If you need to paint the nose remember that white, red and yellow make the best flesh colour, and in order to use a small amount of paint always ADD red and yellow to white.

38

MILKMAID
(Plate III)

An eighteenth-century outfit that would make a good basis for many nursery rhyme characters.

> For mob cap: Enough fine white cotton fabric to make a circle 15½ inches (39·5 cm.) in diameter and a frill 2½ inches (6·5 cm.) wide × 36 inches (90 cm.) long. Broderie Anglaise or ribbon, 1 inch (2·5 cm.) wide × 22 inches (56 cm.) long
>
> For blouse: ½ yard (45 cm.) of muslin
>
> For bodice: ⅜ yard (34·5 cm.) each of black heavy rayon and black Staflex iron-on stiffening for lining (for minimum sewing you could use thick black felt). Laces
>
> For apron: ⅜ yard (34·5 cm.) pale blue cotton fabric and 1½ yards (1·4 m.) of upholstery ribbon
>
> For skirts: One end of old sheet dyed mid-blue
>
> For bucket: cardboard boxes

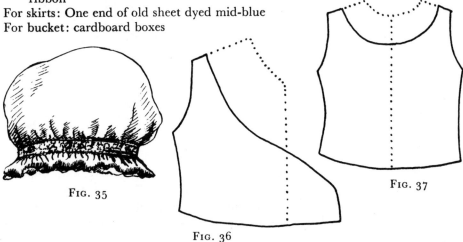

FIG. 35

FIG. 36

FIG. 37

Mob cap   Cut circle of fabric 15½ inches (39·5 cm.) in diameter and oversew round edge. Join ends of broderie anglaise together, and gather up edge of circle to the same measurement (i.e. about 22 inches (56 cm.)). Sew them together. Oversew and gather up frill. Join to other side of broderie Anglaise. See Fig. 35.

Blouse   Adapt a basic bodice shape as Figs. 36 and 37. No darts are necessary. To cut a pattern for collar, place back and front patterns together so that shoulder seams overlap (see Fig. 38). Draw curve of collar as shown and cut out in double thickness of material. Sew outside edges together, turn inside out and press flat before sewing on to blouse. Cut three-quarter-length sleeves quite plain but with turn-back cuffs.

Bodice   Should be made to fit fairly snugly. It can be adjusted to fit quite a wide

39

range of sizes with the laced-up front. Put two darts in the front and two darts in the back as shown in Fig. 39. Join all seams of both bodice and lining. Place lining on to bodice so that the 'right' sides are inside. All seams and darts should have been well pressed open. Sew right round neck, front and waist edge. Turn inside out by way of one of the armhole openings. Press this seam flat and then sew armhole edges in by hand. Make your eyelet holes with the correct gadget if you can get hold of one. Otherwise cut small holes with the help of a skewer and sharp-pointed scissors. Stop edges fraying with Copydex. Thread through a pair of children's black shoelaces.

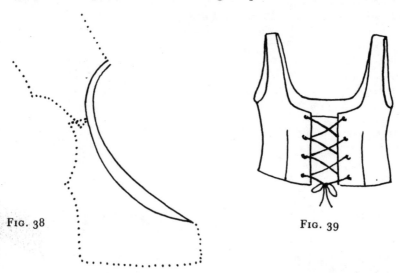

FIG. 38   FIG. 39

Apron   Make a simple square apron say 14 inches (35·5 cm.) long × 18 inches (45 cm.) wide. Turn ½ inch (1·5 cm.) in round hem and sides, and cover edge with decorative ribbon. Also sew another length of ribbon along hem 2½ inches (6·5 cm.) away from bottom. Gather up along waist and sew on to apron strings which should measure about 1¼ yards (1·1 m.).

Skirts   These are simply a long gathered length of material wrapped two or three times round child's waist. If you make them fairly long they will last your child quite a few years, so take a measurement from the waist to the ankles. Cut a width of this length off an old sheet. Use the hem-stitched edge for the hem of the skirt. Take the opposite edge and gather it up as much as possible. Make a long belt as follows. Cut a 1¾-yards (1·6-m.) length of sheet about 3 inches (7·5 cm.) wide (1½-yards (1·4-m.) length will be enough if it is a single sheet). Pin gathered skirt length on to centre of this strip and sew up ends that are left to make two ties (see Fig. 12, page 24). Turn inside out and press flat. Next sew in skirt, first down one side, and then down the other. It is now ready to dye blue (if you want). Remember these points. Have the skirt thoroughly wet, and the dye powder absolutely dissolved. Have as large a bowl

III. MILKMAID AND NURSE

as possible to do the boiling in, and once you have immersed whatever you are dyeing NEVER stop agitating it around with an old wooden spoon.

Milk pail   Use cardboard and not corrugated board. See Chapter 2 for using card. Cut out for main part of pail a piece 9 inches (23 cm.) × 24½ inches (62 cm.); two strips 25 inches (63·5 cm.) × 1 inch (2·5 cm.) wide, and two strips 23 inches (58·5 cm.) long × 1 inch (2·5 cm.) wide. Wrap the main piece round itself so that it overlaps an inch (2·5 cm.), making a cylinder, and fix in place with a staple top and bottom. Cover edge with strips of brown sticky paper on the outside and inside. Take one of the longer strips and putting some P.V.A. glue down one side, wrap round the bottom edge of cylinder so that it sticks. Keep it secure with a couple of staples on the join. Take one of the shorter length strips and glue it round on the inside of cylinder at the same edge. Cut out a circle of cardboard 7⅜ inches (18·5 cm.) in diameter, put some glue round edge, and drop inside, so that it rests on top of the strip. Put the two other strips round top edge in the same way as the bottom. To make handle cut two pieces 7 inches (18 cm.) long × 1½ inches (4 cm.) wide. Stick them together and round off corners. Stick on to pail where shown adding staples for extra strength. Paint inside with white emulsion paint.

NURSE
(Plate III)

For apron: White cotton sheet fabric, 1 yard (90 cm.) white tape, 2 gold safety pins
Mask and cuffs: Muslin or cambric
Cap: Stiffened muslin or paper
Belt: Belt stiffening and part of old door handle for silver buckle
Extras: School frock. Black stockings for winter

Apron   Should be strong and sturdy because nurses have a lot of hard work to do. I have made mine in two separate pieces, both with double thickness. The following size would fit the 6–9-year age group. The upper part 7 inches (18 cm.) length × 6½ inches (16·5 cm.) width. The lower part 16½ inches (42 cm.) length × 13 inches (33 cm.) width (increasing to 16 inches (40·5 cm.) at hem). Allow ½ inch (1·5 cm.) turnings all round, and 2 inches (5 cm.) at hem. Sew all round side seams and hem. Turn inside out, press with iron, and top stitch. Join top half to bottom and attach 1½ feet (45 cm.) of tape each side for tying round waist. Fix on safety pins in readiness for use.

Mask   Cut a piece of fabric 6½ inches (16·5 cm.) × 4½ inches (11·5 cm.) (this includes turnings). Cut darts out each side (see Fig. 40) about 2 inches (5 cm.) long and ½ inch (1·5 cm.) deep and sew down. Sew 6½ inches (16·5 cm.) of shearing elastic each end to fix round ears.

42

Cuffs Cut out two pieces of fabric, 18 inches (45 cm.) long × 4 inches (10 cm.) wide (including turnings). Join ends together. Oversew edges, sew ½ inch (1·5 cm.) from edge all round with shearing elastic to gather up material as much as possible.

Cap (A) The one shown in the illustration (Plate III) is an old-fashioned cap, the sort worn by Victorian women in many different types of service, such as nursemaids, parlour maids, waitresses, etc. The long ties flowing from the back of the cap look very pretty. For headband cut a strip of material 2½ inches (6·5 cm.) wide × 24 inches (60 cm.) long and for the ties two pieces 2½ inches (6·5 cm.) wide, increasing to 4 inches (10 cm.) × 14 inches (35·5 cm.) long. Seam the ties to each end of the headband, then sew side edges together, leaving a large enough gap to turn inside

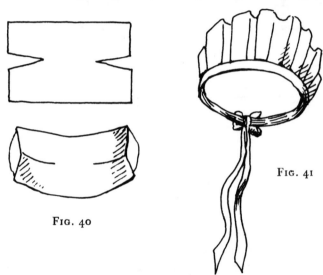

FIG. 40

FIG. 41

out. Press flat and sew up gap. Cut material for the frill 24 inches (60 cm.) in length and 3½ inches (9 cm.) in width. Round off corners down one side and hem down outside edge. Make about fourteen small pleats and sew on to headband (see Fig. 41).

Cap (B) A modern nurse's cap. You will need a piece of smooth white paper 13 inches (33 cm.) × 8 inches (20·5 cm.). Cut out to shape as Fig. 42. Make creases between x's as indicated. Join edges AB to CD so that they overlap nearly an inch (2·5 cm.), and keep together with a few spots of glue. Keep cap fixed in place with kirbigrips.

Belt Measure child's waist and add 1½ inches (4 cm.) overlap each end. Cut your belt stiffening to this length and round off all edges. Paint all over one side a good bright blue. Sew an inch (2·5 cm.) piece of Velcro each end and sew on ornamental silver buckle (or something that looks like one).

43

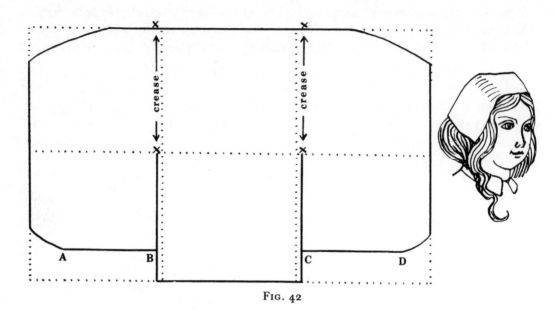

FIG. 42

MEDIAEVAL PRINCESS
(Plate IV)

If this dress is to look like a real princess's dress, it should certainly trail a little on the ground. The difficulty will be that children grow so fast, and in less than six months the hem-line will be up to the child's ankles. I suggest you add a very large hem-line, which is easily let down, and take into consideration the various dangers that a child in a long skirt may be subject to.

For dress: A pale blue silky fabric, 1¼ yards (1·1 m.) for sleeves and bodice and 2 yards (1·8 m.) for skirt (up to 7 and 8 years); 1 yard (90 cm.) of silver and blue braid for sleeves

For brocaded over-garment: ½ yard (45 cm.) of rich-looking silver fabric

For girdle: 1½ yards (1·4 m.) of 1 inch (2·5 cm.) wide decorative trimming (I have made mine from a strip of the brocade which I dyed blue to match cord); 1 yard (90 cm.) of rich blue silk cord

For coronet and veil: Cardboard and gold paper or paint spray. Blue and green shiny paper for jewels; ⅝ yard (57 cm.) gold upholstery cord; ⅝ yard (57 cm.) of fine flimsy fabric

Dress Cut a simple bodice down to fairly low on the hip-line (3½ inches (9 cm.) below waist for small children and 4½ inches (11·5 cm.) for bigger ones). Darts are not needed, but make a six-inch (15-cm.) slit down front for head to go through, and

44

IV. MEDIAEVAL PRINCESS

finish it with facing or bias binding. Cut sleeves 18 inches (45 cm.) wide. Measure armpit to wrist and add 14 inches (35·5 cm.) for point (see Fig. 43). Make gathering stitches where shown, on dotted lines, taking in width from 9 to 11 inches (23 to 28 cm.) depending on child's arm measurement. Stitch down binding on top of gathering stitches, join seam edges and oversew bottom of sleeve. Cut your pattern for skirt as follows. First take measurements down centre front, from waist to floor, and from this subtract waist to hip measurement (already established for the bodice); also measure round hips. Take some large sheets of newspaper (it will be necessary to Sellotape them together) and using the corner as your right angle, draw half hip measurement plus 1 inch (2·5 cm.) as shown in Fig. 44. Make the line slightly

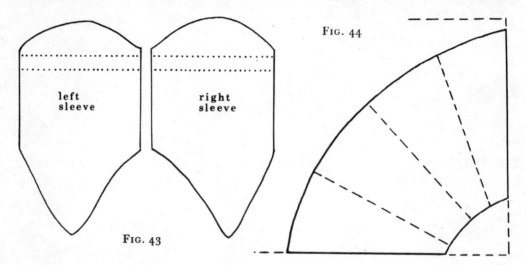

FIG. 44

left
sleeve

right
sleeve

FIG. 43

curved. From this measure off the length of the skirt from several points. Draw in curve. Cut out two pieces from this pattern, one for the front the other for the back. Sew up side seams and sew on to bodice leaving a gap down left-hand side for a zip. Sew in sleeves, and finish off hem.

Overgarment Cut out in exactly the same shape as dress bodice, and make neck opening in front as before, facing it with the same fabric. I have sewn mine directly on to the dress in order to simplify the process of getting dressed. It will also be necessary to use only one zip fastener if you do it this way.

Girdle If you wish to make one from the same material as the overgarment cut a 2-inch (5-cm.) wide strip to the same length as the hip plus the waist measurements and sew it down on to a 1-inch (2·5 cm.) wide piece of petersham or thick corded ribbon of the same length. Dye it blue. Cut your length of cord in half. Sew to either end of girdle to make two ties. Unravel 4 inches (10 cm.) out each end, knot tightly and comb out.

46

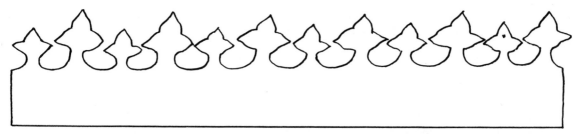

FIG. 45

Coronet Measure round crown of head, and take a length of strong but flexible cardboard at least 4 inches (10 cm.) wide and about 24 inches (60 cm.) long. If you wish to use gold paper follow direction (a). If you intend to use a gold paint spray follow direction (b).

(a) Cut your gold paper the same length as the cardboard but double the width. Glue thoroughly all over one side of cardboard and cover with one half of the gold paper. Press down firmly. Then turn over and glue other side of cardboard and folding gold paper carefully over one long edge of it press down so that the paper is now stuck both sides. Keep the edge that is covered intact, and on the other edge draw six large foliated shapes and six small ones as in Fig. 45. Add an inch (2·5 cm.) one end for a join, cut shape out, and glue round with Evo-Stik. Measure the gold braid round and stick down with Copydex. Cut out the jewels in shiny paper. Make the oval ones about 1 inch (2·5 cm.) long, and the round ones $\frac{5}{8}$ inch (16 mm.) in diameter (see Fig. 46). Stick beneath each leaf-shape.

(b) Draw the foliated shapes on the cardboard and cut out with a very sharp knife. Stick the overlapping end piece round with Evo-Stik. Measure braid (it can be any colour) and stick down. Spray gold paint all over coronet, inside and out. Stick down paper jewels as in direction (a).

Veil Oversew or zigzag the raw edges of your material. The selvedges are used to make the sides of the veil. Gather one length together very closely and stick inside coronet with Copydex.

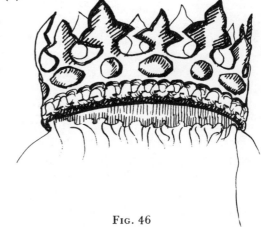

FIG. 46

CRUSADER
(Plate V)

Boys are fascinated by all sorts of armour, and since dressing up for them is usually combined with some particular activity, outfits of this sort are very popular and offer the most scope. Unfortunately the most coveted suit of all, the full plate armour of the fourteenth and fifteenth centuries, is much too difficult to make, but a chain mail suit as illustrated in Plate V is quite successful and can be combined with plastic armour if wanted. It consists of three separate garments. The hood (coif) which is rather like a balaclava. The shirt (hauberk) which has mittens attached at the wrist, and, to be authentic, should reach to the knees but can be made shorter for the sake of economy. The leggings (chausse) which have very pointed toes.

The heraldic symbols on the surcoat, shield and horse were a means of identifying a knight in battle, and it would be good to suggest to your knight that he looks in a few books on heraldry and chooses some emblems that he would like to wear on his outfit.

> For chain mail suit: For your material choose a fabric that imitates silk crochet work, in a pale colour. Black dye. (Quantity depends on age of child and width of fabric so make the patterns first and take assessment from them—approx. 2½ yards (2·3 m.).)
> For helm, sword and shield: Cardboard (not corrugated board)
> For surcoat: Old white sheet. Felt for heraldic emblem
> For belt and scabbard: ¼ yard (23 cm.) leather-cloth
> Extras: Flexible innersoles for feet (a size or two too big). Red, white and gold paints. Silver paint spray

Chain mail suit Firstly, make your patterns. The shirt is a T-shaped garment (see Figs. 47 and 10) and if your material is wide (42 inches (1m.) to 48 inches (1·2 m.) for instance) you will be able to cut it in one piece to the wrist. If it is only 36 inches (90 cm.) in width, you must cut sleeves separately from armhole position. Also cut mitten pieces to sew at wrist. Garment should come a few inches above knees and can be fairly loose fitting. The leg covering pattern should be cut as narrow fitting trousers but extra added for the feet (see Fig. 48). The hood patterns can be made from the measurements given in the illustration (Fig. 49, a and b), unless it is for a child under six in which case I should reduce it slightly all round.

Next dye your material black, leaving it in dye-bath just until it becomes a dark charcoal-grey. You will be surprised how this will make the fabric quite metallic looking. Hang material up to dry.

48

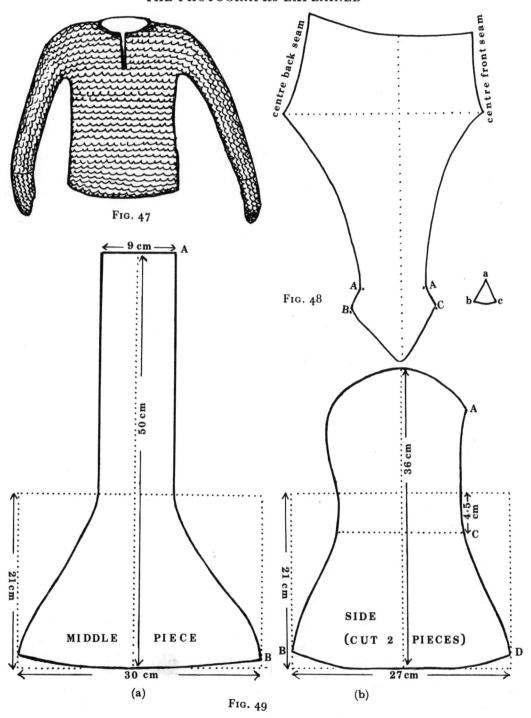

FIG. 47

FIG. 48

centre back seam

centre front seam

A
B
A
C

a
b   c

9 cm — A

50 cm

21 cm

30 cm

MIDDLE   PIECE

B

(a)

36 cm

A

4·5 cm

C

21 cm

27 cm

SIDE
(CUT 2 PIECES)

B

D

FIG. 49

(b)

Cut out pieces and sew seams together as unobtrusively as possible.

Make the shirt up as follows Stitch mittens to sleeves at wrist line. Then stitch all along side seams and round end of mittens. Cut a slit 2½ inches (6·5 cm.) down centre front for head to go through. Oversew round neck and hem-line edges. Join opening together with narrow leather-cloth lacing.

Make the leggings as follows Seam together centre back and front seams. Join inside leg seam to within 1½ inches (4 cm.) of bottom of heel at point A. Sew a small triangle for heel matching points A, B and C. Then sew foot on to innersoles, having first cut them to sharp points. To make a good strong walking surface for underneath of foot, stick down another sole of felt or leather. Machine edge at waist over an inch (2·5 cm.) and thread elastic through to keep leggings up.

Sew hood as follows Join one side piece to the middle piece between points A and B. Join the other outside piece on to the opposite side. Sew together the outside pieces between points C and D to join hood underneath chin. Oversew round outside edges if necessary or Copydex them to prevent fraying.

Helm Cut out Fig. 50 and Fig. 51 in thick cardboard. The size given will do for all ages. Cut away shaded areas in the circular piece for crown and then join the darts together, by the following method, to give a curved ellipse for the crown. Cut short strips of sticky brown paper and holding the two edges of a dart together put sticky paper across on inside to hold it together. Allow to dry completely and then cover closed up dart on outside with a sticky strip of paper. Do the same with the three remaining darts. On the other piece of cardboard cut out slits for eyes and holes for breathing, where indicated. Join edge AB to CD and stick together with sticky tape, so that the top is fairly circular. Stick crown on top with a strong glue. For a perfect finish, papier mâché all over with small pieces of tissue paper (you can work round the eyes but you will have to prod open the small holes with a pencil) and finally spray all over with silver paint when the papier mâché is quite dry.

Surcoat Measure child from shoulder to a few inches above ankles. Cut a piece of sheet double that length and 24 inches (60 cm.) wide. Measure child again from shoulder to hips. See Fig. 52. Cut a narrow opening for head in centre and cut opening in front as marked. Oversew down two side edges, two centre opening edges and round neckline. Fold in half down shoulder line and leaving an armhole of 8 inches (20·5 cm.) in length sew down side seams. Hem round bottom. Sew elastic tight round waistline to gather it in. Run gathering stitches along both shoulders to reduce them to about 2½ inches (6·5 cm.) long. Cut out heraldic emblem in felt. For speed stick it down with Copydex, or for a better finish zigzag edges with a machine.

V. CRUSADER

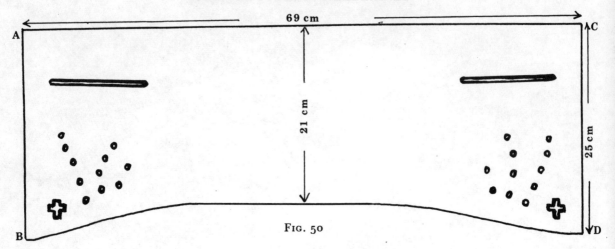

A ← 69 cm → C

21 cm

25 cm

B   FIG. 50   D

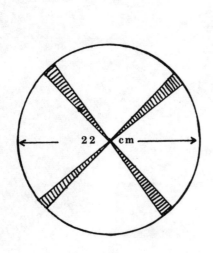

← 2 2 cm →

FIG. 51

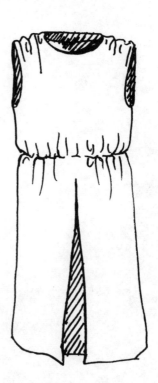

FIG. 52

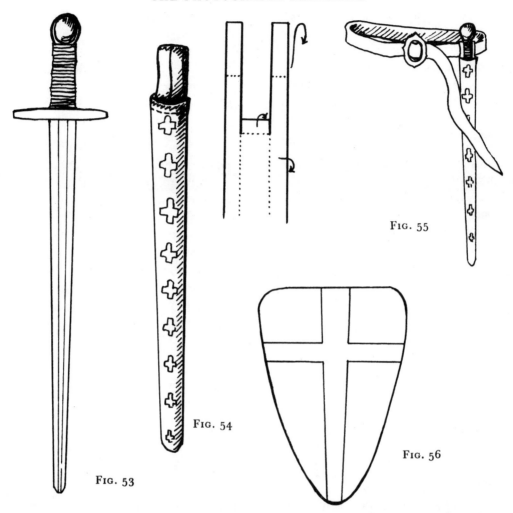

FIG. 55

FIG. 54

FIG. 56

FIG. 53

Sword See Fig. 53. Stage 1. Cut two or three pieces of cardboard (depending on thickness) about 27 inches (68·5 cm.) in overall length and stick them together. Cut two narrow strips and stick them in centre on either side. Stage 2. Cut two pieces to make hilt and glue them in place on either side of blade. Select two caps, plastic or metal, just under 2 inches (5 cm.) across, from jars on the kitchen shelves and stick them facing together to make pommel. Wind some string round and round handle and secure in place. Papier mâché over blade and pommel and glue all over string handle. Paint black all over and then spray lightly with silver paint.

Scabbard and belt Draw the shape of the sword up to the hilt on some light cardboard. Add ⅛ inch (3 mm.) all round. Cut out. Mark this shape on some leathercloth, double its width for side pieces to wrap around back and add 1½ inches (4 cm.)

on top of them to be sewn on to belt. See Fig. 54. Turn over edges as indicated by dotted lines. Wrap it round cardboard and glue side edges on to back of cardboard so that sword fits snugly inside. The flap is free to be sewn into belt. Cut your belt as long as the width of your leather-cloth and 3½ inches (9 cm.) in width. Glue it together so that the two edges meet together round the inside of the belt. Cut a medieval type buckle in two layers of very strong cardboard, paint it blackish silver, and sew on to belt. Sew on scabbard and embellish both with plenty of gilt decoration. Place sword inside. See Fig. 55.

Shield 24 inches (60 cm.) in length by 16 inches (40 cm.) at widest point. Cut a curved triangular shape as illustrated (Fig. 56). Brush all over with Polycell paste and when card starts to soften curve edges inwards so that shield becomes slightly concave and will curve round body. Do not overwork wet cardboard or it will start to crack. When you are satisfied with the shape, wedge shield in that position and leave to dry. Cut out a piece of cardboard (or corrugated card would do here) about 4 inches (10 cm.) wide at top, tapering to 2½ inches (6·5 cm.) and glue down centre at back of shield to give it extra strength. Stick a piece of bent card for arm to go through at back, see Fig. 63, page 57, and paint on any heraldic motifs you like in rich, bright colours.

INDO-PERSIAN WARRIOR
(Plate VI)

For chain mail shirt: Make exactly as for Crusader
For tunic: A piece of old sheet dyed a rose colour
For helmet, breastplate and armplates: Cardboard (not corrugated board) and leather or webbing for straps. Black, silver and gold lacquer paint
For shield: Thick corrugated cardboard and an egg-box
Extras: Cheap red plastic sandals (Oriental type)

Make a chain mail shirt exactly like Crusader's, except it may be dyed a darker grey and decorated with gold patterns round neckline and hem-line.

Tunic Measure child from shoulder to mid-calf. Cut a rather narrow T-shaped garment with short sleeves, that flares slightly at hem as shown in Fig. 57. Sew together down side seams. Cut an opening for head about 6½ inches (16·5 cm.) across, and an opening down centre front about 5½ inches (14 cm.) long, which should be hemmed down. Cut a collar 13 inches (33 cm.) in length and 4 inches (10 cm.) wide (this does not include seam allowances), double over down length and sew together at ends. Stitch to neckline. Hem round sleeves and bottom edge. Dye tunic a dark rose pink and paint on some stripes round hem and collar in gold lacquer.

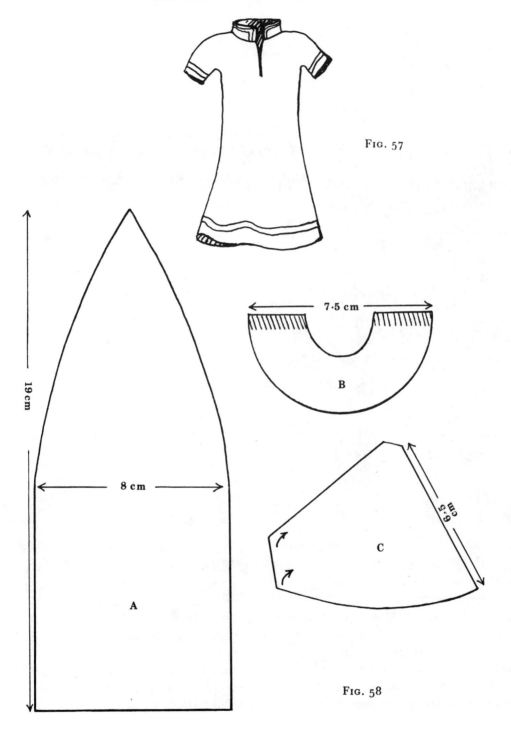

Fig. 57

19 cm

8 cm

A

7·5 cm

B

6·5 cm

C

Fig. 58

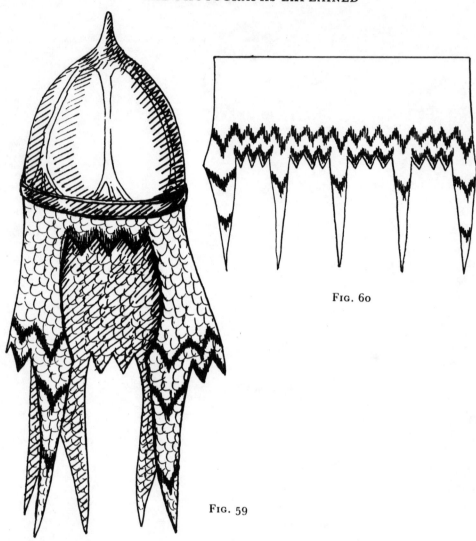

FIG. 60

FIG. 59

Helmet Cut seven sections as pattern A, Fig. 58, using same measurements if child's head measures under 21 inches (53.5 cm.) round largest part. (If bigger add width accordingly on each section.) Glue edges together, section by section, adding masking tape on inside to give extra strength and stability. It may help to dampen cardboard and mould it before you begin the sticking operation, but you will have to wait until sections are quite dry, otherwise the glue will not adhere properly. When parts are firmly stuck add a 1½ inch (4 cm.) wide cardboard strip round bottom and while it is drying, press and wedge helmet into an oval shape, to fit the head more comfortably. Using card from a cereal pack, cut out pattern B and pattern C. First

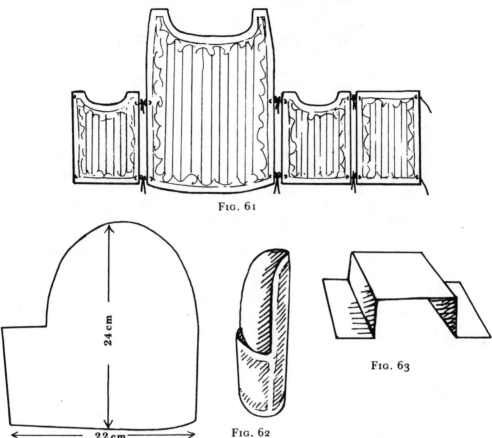

FIG. 61

24 cm

22 cm

FIG. 62

FIG. 63

take part B and gluing it all over wrap it round so that shaded areas overlap a little. Stick it down on top of helmet, moulding it with your fingertips. Next take part C and roll it round and round so that tip is tight together and base fits snugly into part B. Unroll and glue all over, then roll up again as before. Set into centre of B. Paint helmet black all over and when it is quite dry, run some very diluted silver paint over it so that you achieve the effect of a very dark metal. Cut out a length of your chain mail material (see Fig. 59), and stick it round with Copydex, also gluing round edges of chain mail to prevent fraying. Paint on gold decoration as the shaded area (Fig. 60).

Breastplate and body armour This goes right round body in four sections, each linked with leather straps. There is a front, two side pieces and a back (see Fig. 61). Cut out parts and dampen with a little water. Curve into shape to fit round body. When dry paint in same method as the helmet, and lastly stick on the shoulder straps and tying laces.

VI. INDO-PERSIAN WARRIOR AND ROMAN SOLDIER

Armplates Draw a pattern from Fig. 62 and fit to check size. Cut out in card and dampen. Curve round to form a cylinder and tie round string to keep it in place. When dry, it should remain in place. Paint as the rest of the armour.

Shield Cut out a circle of thick corrugated card about 14 inches (35·5 cm.) across. Stick on five sections of an egg box. Mix some Polyfilla to a soft consistency and rub all over surface, especially filling in the hollow corrugated edge. Paint black, silver and gold as before. Cut a piece of the corrugated board 13 inches (33 cm.) long and 4½ inches (11·5 cm.) wide. Score and crease where indicated in Fig. 63. Stick on back of shield for hand hold.

ROMAN SOLDIER
(Plate VI)

Caution: this outfit is not completely accurate. Most of it belongs to an ordinary Roman legionary, but the plumed helmet and sword belt are those of an officer in the Praetorian guard. If authenticity is required you should refer to a costume book, but for everyday purposes a boy will be quite pleased with this one.

> For tunic and scarf: Red cotton fabric, about 1½ yards (1·4 m.)
> For cloak: A rectangle measuring about 54 inches (1·4 m.) × 20 inches (51 cm.) of coarse wool material in off-white or red
> For body armour (cuirass): Cardboard and leather (leather-cloth or webbing)
> For helmet: An old felt hat, cardboard and silk or cotton cord
> For horse-hair plume: brown feather duster or sizal string
> Sword-belt (baldrick) and sword: Cardboard and leather-cloth
> Extras: Red knee-length socks. Bronze paint spray

Tunic Measure child from shoulder to mid-calf. Cut a T-shaped garment with this measurement for length and width from sleeve to sleeve. See Fig. 64. Cut an opening for the head to go through about 7½ inches (19 cm.) in width. Finish this circular edge with a narrow strip cut on the bias. Sew down side seams, and hem-stitch round sleeves and bottom of tunic. For scarf to tie round neck cut a piece on the bias about 36 inches (90 cm.) long and 5 inches (12·5 cm.) wide with pointed ends, hem-stitch all round.

Cloak Hem-stitch any raw edges of rectangle and gather up on to shoulder with a plain gold brooch (or a nappy pin).

Body armour This was made of hinged metal strips that fitted round the body, with leather straps hanging from waist and shoulders for extra protection. The following measurements would probably fit most boys up to the age of 8 or 9, but they are

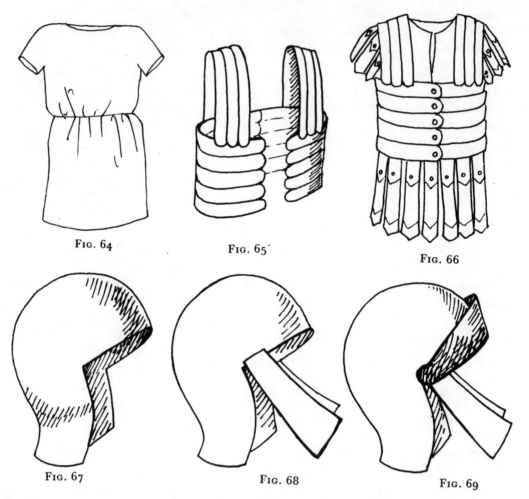

FIG. 64

FIG. 65

FIG. 66

FIG. 67

FIG. 68

FIG. 69

only given as a guide line. Cut a strip of cardboard and place very loosely round body to give you an accurate measure of what length you ought to cut.

(a) Strips to go round body are $1\frac{3}{8}$ inches (3·5 cm.) wide and 14 inches (35·5 cm.) long. There are five each side, making a total of ten. They are fixed together with glue at the centre back, and left open in the front.

(b) Strips to go over shoulders are 1 inch (2·5 cm.) wide. There are three each side, making a total of six. The two nearest to the arms measure $15\frac{1}{2}$ inches (39·5 cm.) in length. The two centre ones measure 16 inches (40·5 cm.) in length, and the two nearest the neckline measure $16\frac{1}{2}$ inches (42 cm.) in length.

All the strips have rounded ends. Dampen each one, and mould them to shape round body, i.e. a very narrow curve (see Fig. 65). Wedge them to keep their shape, while they are still damp, and leave them to dry overnight.

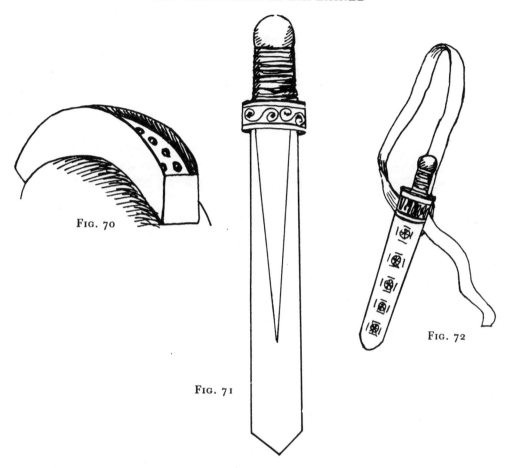

FIG. 70

FIG. 71

FIG. 72

Stick the (a) strips together with a very strong contact adhesive like Evo-Stick overlapping edges as little as possible. Join them together at centre back and glue a few pieces of Velcro down front overlapping sections to join armour together in the front.

Glue the (b) strips together in the same way and test on child for positioning before you stick them on to the main body part. Stick some plain buttons (no holes) down front and spray all over with bronze paint. Cut out pieces of leather, or something that looks like it (see Fig. 66), and stick them round shoulder and waist edges. Paint on some decoration with gold paint.

Helmet Roman helmets are absolutely rounded on top, and there is no easy way of making this shape out of materials such as cardboard. I have made mine from an old felt hat, and I am sure if you keep a look-out you will also be able to find a suitable one that has no other useful purpose left. First of all cut it into a basic helmet shape as Fig. 67, then brush it all over with diluted P.V.A. glue and papier mâché over surface with tissue paper. Allow to dry rock hard. Cut out two cheek pieces in cardboard (see Fig. 68), and glue in place. Next, cut out forehead piece in cardboard (see Fig. 69), and also glue in place. Snake some pieces of cord round into patterns and stick down with P.V.A. to look like ornamental metal work. Paint all over bronze, and thread two lengths of leather thonging through cheek pieces to tie under the chin.

Plume   Make a cardboard base to hold plumes in place. The curve must match the curve of your helmet so that it may be glued down without any gaps. It should measure nearly 9 inches (23 cm.) in length and 1 inch (2·5 cm.) in width (see Fig. 70), and a section should be stuck inside about ¼ inch (6 mm.), as shown with holes bored through it to secure the feathers or string in place. Stick base on to helmet, decorate with cord, and paint all over bronze. Glue feathers into holes, or lengths of string that have been combed out and dyed brown.

Sword belt and sword   Cut a long belt measuring about 50 inches (1·3 m.) in length and 2 inches (5 cm.) in width. Trim one end to a V-shape and turn the other end over 2½ inches (6·5 cm.) and machine down, so that you have a loop which the belt can be threaded through. Decorate with gold patterns. Make a sword and scabbard by the same method as the Crusader but make the sword shorter and wider (22 inches (56 cm.) long) (see Fig. 71) and do not make a flap on the scabbard. Stick loop of belt on the top of the scabbard at the back, so that belt may be draped over left shoulder, under right arm, and drawn through loop (see Fig. 72).

Footgear   Cut long, long strips of leather-cloth, and do them up, criss-cross fashion, over some knee length socks.

COWBOY
(Plate VII)

I suppose every boy at one time or another acquires some of the trappings of a cowboy; either the holster and guns, or the hat, or quite probably both. This is the prime character to thrill boys of all ages, and all cultures seem to identify easily with him—the lone herdsman, galloping with his cattle across the wide-open plains. As most commercial outfits represent modern American circus cowboys, I suggest that you try a traditional approach for a change. The only clothes I have made especially for the outfit photographed in Plate VII are the leather chaps. These are the over-trousers worn by cowboys to save their trousers from wearing out with the long hours spent in the saddle. They are quite simply made out of leather-cloth. Other things needed are as follows:

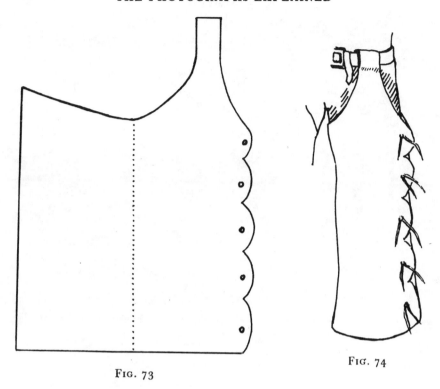

FIG. 73

FIG. 74

Felt cowboy hat: Press the brim with a hot iron and a wet cloth so that the front and
    back are curled up for a change, rather than the two sides
Shirt: A very dark coloured one looks best, but a check Viyella type will also look
    authentic
Scarf: A traditional workman's spotted handkerchief
Extras: Black braces, corduroy jeans, boots, a gun and holster belt

Leather chaps Measure child from hips, and calculate yardage as follows—say, for
example, that the length measurement is ¾ yard (68·5 cm.), then if the material is
48 inches (1·2 m.) wide, that length will be enough, but if it is 36 inches (90 cm.) or
under wide, you must buy double the quantity, i.e. 1½ yards (1·4 m.).

They are made in two separate pieces, like a pair of trousers that haven't been
joined together. You must remember to cut out the two pieces the opposite way
round (otherwise you will have two left legs). Cut the eyelet holes where shown on
the flaps (Fig. 73), and sew or stick down narrow strips of leather to tie the sides
together (Fig. 74). Sew a loop on top to thread holster belt through. This keeps the
chaps on round hips.

VII. COWBOY AND RED INDIAN CHIEFTAIN

RED INDIAN CHIEFTAIN
(Plate VII)

As with commercial cowboy clothes, the Red Indian outfits you buy in shops are sometimes a far cry from the real ones worn by American Indians. If you are making some yourself, it is certainly worth referring to pictures and photographs of actual Indian people, and although animal skins and bead-work are not within the scope of many people, at least one can try and use the correct colours and designs. You will have to use a material that looks like smooth pale leather. Indian chieftains' garments were often made from beautiful antelope skins, which is a soft almost white leather.

If you want to make a squaw's dress for a girl, carry out the directions for the shirt below, but do not include the sleeves and extend the hem-line down to an inch or two above the ankles. Paint on the traditional Indian patterns and give her a simple 1 inch (2·5 cm.) wide leather headband with one or two feathers sticking up, back or front.

> For shirt, trousers and tobacco pouch: I have used fawn curtain lining sateen which looks effectively like leather. Quantity depends on age of child. Add together measurements from shoulder to mid-thigh and waist to ankle. Add another ¾ yard (68·5 cm.) (approx. 2½ yards (2·3 m.) for a 9–10-year-old)
>
> For head-dress: Use large turkey feathers to look like eagle feathers (only obtainable at Christmas time). If unavailable use a brown feather duster which has a smaller variety of turkey feathers; ¼ yard (23 cm.) of white swansdown; ½ yard (45 cm.) lengths of scarlet, pink and lemon coloured ribbon; 1 yard (90 cm.) of 2-inch (5-cm.) wide webbing
>
> Extras: Indian bead-necklaces, a pipe, and moccasins. Poster paint, in dark brown, red, earth, yellow ochre, dull green

Shirt Cut a loose T-shaped garment without any sleeves (see Fig. 75). Cut a curve for neckline measuring 9 inches (23 cm.) across. Sew down side seams leaving a 6½ inch (16·5 cm.) length gap for sleeves. Cut sleeves to measure 12 inches (30 cm.) wide all the way down, to the required length. Next make your fringes. Cut long strips of the material about 4 inches (10 cm.) wide. Mix a thin, watery solution of P.V.A. glue, brush carefully all over and leave to dry. Cut a narrow fringe (¼ inch (6 mm.)) all the way down.

Sew this fringing between the seamed edges of your sleeves (see Fig. 76) which will run down the outside of the arm. Cut a slit 2½ inches (6·5 cm.) long for under-arm of sleeve and insert a triangular piece of fabric, 2½ inches (6·5 cm.) wide at base. Sew sleeve into armhole with another length of fringe to fall over shoulder (see Fig. 77). Sew about five feathers round neckline and finish edge with a narrow strip of material cut on the bias. Hem-stitch round sleeves and hem-line. Paint on patterns.

Trousers Cut trousers to fit fairly loosely and sew a length of fringing down each side seam.

Tobacco pouch Make a small bag about 5½ inches (14 cm.) wide by 7 inches (18 cm.) long. Sew two flaps at the top through which a narrow belt can be threaded in order for it to hang from waist. Paint the beads on in the traditional bright colours of red, blue, green, yellow, white and brown, with felt tip pens. Cut out a piece of thick white cotton material and this will represent the white beads. Draw small circles all over in dark brown and then fill in with your colours in various Indian patterns (see Plate VII).

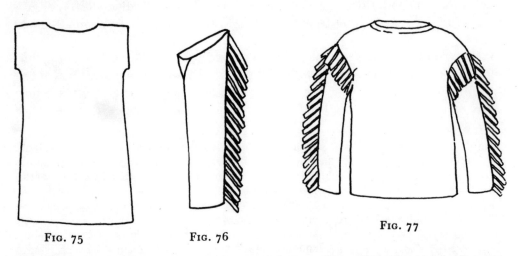

FIG. 75   FIG. 76   FIG. 77

Head-dress To make something rather grand you will need feathers at least 10–12 inches (25·5–30 cm.) long, so if yours are rather small stick two together with P.V.A. glue to make one long one, and repeat the process fifteen times. Cut the swansdown into nine pieces and carefully stick them on to the nine largest feathers about ½ inch (1·5 cm.) from the base. With the webbing make a band to fit closely round the head, folding it in half to make double thickness, and with the open edges kept uppermost so that the feathers may be glued in between them. Cut two strips about 8 inches (20·5 cm.) long, double them down the length, sewing the ends in a diagonal. Glue or sew them on to the band about 3 inches (7·5 cm.) apart, at a slight angle (see Fig. 78). In the drawing you can also see the positioning of the feathers marked by the spots.

Stick the nine best feathers round the front and continue on down with the remainder. Stick on lengths of ribbon each side, by the ears, and make a painted beaded strip (as for the tobacco pouch) to cover all over the webbing band. See Fig. 79.

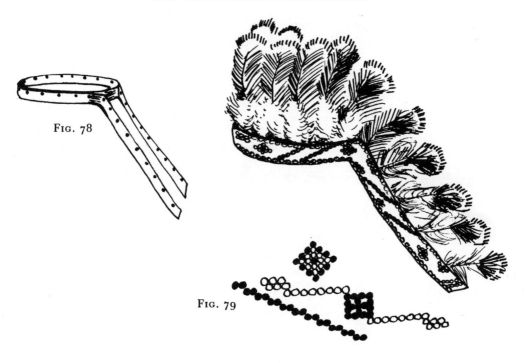

FIG. 78

FIG. 79

SPACEMAN
(Plate VIII)

When you make a spaceman's suit it will probably only be correct for a very short time. As boys are very particular about details, it is best for them to give you all the up-to-date information that you need. I hope some of it will be applicable to our 1970's space explorer.

> For white moon flight suit: I have used 'Vilene' to give it a slightly unworldly appearance, but this is not as strong as a woven fabric, and as the suit must stand up to hard wear, I recommend you to use white sheeting for main garment, and keep the Vilene only for the straps and pockets. To make a really good job, you could line some of the sheeting suit with Vilene, just to help it make a bulkier shape. Also buy a few inches of White Velcro for all fastenings
> For helmet: Cardboard and transparent film (acetate)
> For equipment: 3 yards (2·7 m.) white webbing. Old boxes, 2 empty washing up-liquid bottles, transparent aquarium tubing. Various caps. Silver paint spray
> Extras: Rubber gloves, wellingtons (painted white?) or plimsolls

Moon suit Using a jumper and a pair of trousers as a guide, cut an all in one suit to very generous proportions. It should be seamed down the centre front and centre back (leave 12-inch (30-cm.) opening for the head to go through at the back) and be

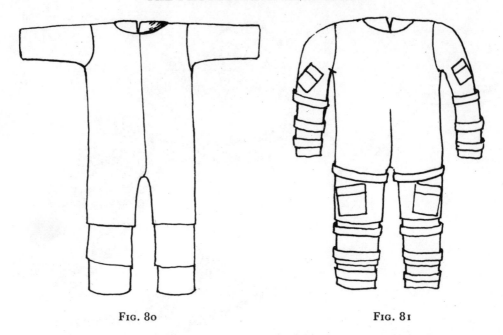

FIG. 80   FIG. 81

made with a few tucks round legs (made by folding fabric before you cut out the shape). The armholes should be cut fairly deep and the sleeves accordingly wide (see Fig. 80). Cut out lots of pockets and straps in Vilene, and sew them on to suit where shown in Fig. 81. Make a belt which may be fixed at the back of the suit and secured with a piece of Velcro in the front. Likewise put Velcro on neck opening at back. If you want to make a flag to give spaceman some nationality, you can paste some coloured material on to a piece of felt and glue it on to suit.

Helmet Cut a piece of cardboard 9 inches (23 cm.) wide by 27 inches (68·5 cm.) in length. Cut a round piece out of centre about 6½ inches (16·5 cm.) across (see Fig.

FIG. 82   FIG. 83

82). Join ends to meet so that they overlap nearly 1½ inches (4 cm.) and fix in place with staples and sticky tape. Cut a circular piece of cardboard 9½ inches (24 cm.) across, and cut a line into centre. Overlap the two edges so that the now formed pyramid shape fits on top of cylinder (see Fig. 83). Stick pyramid together and then stick on to cylinder to make main part of helmet. Paint all over dark blue-black.

Cut out a piece of acetate 9 inches (23 cm.) wide by 27 inches (68·5 cm.) long BUT DO NOT CUT OUT CIRCLE. Wrap round helmet and secure with one or two staples at the base.

Cut a strip of thick cardboard 32 inches (81·5 cm.) long by 1¾ inches (4·5 cm.) wide. Join into a circle, overlapping about 1½ inches (4 cm.), and staple together. (To make an even stronger job cut and make two circles and stick them together.) This circle is now about an inch (2·5 cm.) bigger in circumference all round the base of the helmet and it has to be fixed to it by means of raised cardboard strips. Cut four strips 3 inches (7·5 cm.) × ½ inch (1·5 cm.) and bend them up as in Fig. 63 (page 57). Stick them at centre, back and sides of helmet base, having firstly removed four similar sized strips of acetate, to enable you to glue them more easily on to cardboard. Having sprayed the circle of cardboard with silver paint, now stick it on to the raised strips of cardboard. Glue a white plastic cap on the front.

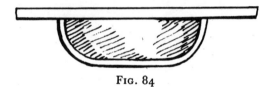

FIG. 84

Make visor as follows. Cut a strip of cardboard 18 inches (45 cm.) long and 1¼ inches (3 cm.) wide. Cut the curved piece 10½ inches (26·5 cm.) across at top and 4½ inches (11·5 cm.) deep (see Fig. 84). Staple on a piece of acetate and glue on to helmet.

Cut a few small breathing holes in acetate at front of helmet.

Equipment
Control pack on chest Find a small cardboard pack from the larder shelf measuring about 6 inches (15 cm.) × 3 inches (7·5 cm.). Stick down on it the top of a 'squeezy' bottle and a plastic cap. Spray all over with silver paint and glue on to front of space suit.

Survival pack worn on back Make a completely enclosed corrugated cardboard box, about 13½ inches (34·5 cm.) long by 10½ inches (26·5 cm.) wide, but do not fix bottom end down yet. Make four slits and thread two 9-inch (23-cm.) lengths of webbing through to inside of box, in order to hold 'squeezy' bottles tightly in place. Glue them down to the inside of the box. Cut a length of webbing to go round box and waist and stick down on back of pack near base. Sew Velcro on ends to fasten it

69

round waist. Cut two strips to go over shoulders. Glue them into slits at top of the box and sew them on to the waist-band in front. Glue the tops of two aerosols at base of pack to prevent 'squeezy' bottles sliding down. See Fig. 85. Seal up bottom end of box. Spray pack, bottles and webbing all over with silver paint spray. Thread aquarium tubing from control pack to survival pack.

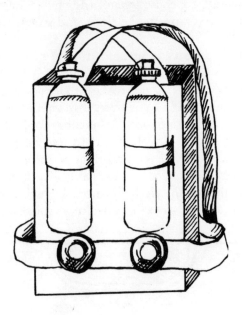

FIG. 85

ROBOT No. 163007,445921
(Plate VIII)

Robots are very easy to make. So much of the manufactured world has become like the parts of a giant robot anyway, and many of the things we throw away all the time seem much too good to waste. It is a good idea to stick them all together and make something both interesting and amusing. You can collect all the things you need from your own home and the local shops. The only thing you need spend money on is a silver paint spray, and it is not absolutely essential that you do that.

No two robots will be alike because the ingredients will vary in every one. The materials shown here are only a rough guide to start you off with ideas of your own. It will be helpful to have a Stanley knife.

For main body: You will need a fairly large box measuring 12 inches (30 cm.) × 12 inches (30 cm.) × 17 inches (43 cm.). Seal it firmly together with brown sticky tape.

VIII. SPACEMAN AND ROBOT

Cut a hole for the head, two armholes, and cut out most of the bottom piece (see Fig. 86)

For head: You will need a box about 9½ inches (24 cm.) square. Cut a square for face, and cut away most of bottom piece

For neck: You will need 2½-inch (6·5-cm.) wide strips of corrugated paper (the soft variety) to make a circle 32 inches (81·5 cm.) in circumference

For arms and legs: Cardboard to form the cylinders, thick elastic to join them to the body, etc.

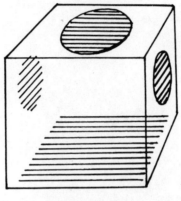

FIG. 86

When your boxes are made and cut, first stick on the corrugated neck to body and then glue on the head. Next, stick any likely paraphernalia all over robot. Here are the things I have used.

On body Weetabix packet with film spools and plastic caps glued to it. Two yoghurt cartons. Paper roll tube. A piece of vacuum formed plastic packaging.

On head Plastic egg tray for eye cells. Two small cereal packs with a section from an egg tray stuck on each, to make the ears. A cake-mix box is glued on top of the head, with a small torch inside which lights up the mousse mould, fixed on the top.

A piece of bicycle inner tube links head to body at the back of the robot. Black Letraset numbers, dots and dashes have been added after it has been sprayed all over with silver paint.

To make the robot more comfortable to wear, I have put inside the body box, where it rests on the shoulders, a piece of thick plastic foam from Woolworth's. This avoids any uncomfortable chafing.

CHAPTER 5

Parties

These outfits are intended to be suitable for putting together quickly, with the minimum bother and expense. Use of existing clothes is made whenever possible.

I have tried to pair a boy's outfit with a girl's when appropriate, and they are roughly arranged so that the easier ones come first.

POLICEMAN

You will need:

One dark blue or black school blazer
Silver milk bottle tops
Chain and whistle
Notebook and pencil
Toy helmet and truncheon (it's not worth making your own)
Any dark long trousers
Schoolboy's belt

Turn up collar of blazer. Wash about twelve milk bottle tops. Cover three blazer buttons pressing well into shape. Make remaining bottle tops into solid buttons. Stitch three in a line above buttonholes, and two on shoulder seams. Choose a number for your policeman and cut two sets of numerals in light card from a cereal packet. Cover numerals in kitchen foil. Sew on to the two ends of the lapel.

Cut arm bands in white cartridge paper. Mark on black stripes with ink or felt-tip pen, and staple or Sellotape both ends together. Attach silver chain to middle chest button and drop into adjacent pocket with a whistle if you have one.

Paint an old snake-buckle belt black to wear round waist, if an old fashioned sort of copper is wanted.

LITTLE RED RIDING HOOD

You will need:
  Red material for cape
  Old brown shopping basket filled with goodies and
    covered with white napkin
  Boots

To make cape, measure length of child from neck to below
the knee. Roughly speaking 2 yards (1·8 m.) of 48 inches
(1·2 m.) width material will be enough for a cape to the
ground for a 4-year-old, and below the knees for a
10-year-old. Find centre of fabric down one of the
selvedge edges and mark with a pin. Measure 5 inches
(12·5 cm.) away from this point on either side and 5 inches (12·5 cm.) towards
the centre and mark these three points. Draw semicircle between these points with
tailor's chalk and cut out. See Fig. 87. From this neckline measure the length and
cut hem-line. From one of the side pieces cut out your hood (see Fig. 88). Sew all
darts as indicated and centre back seam of hood and then join hood to cape. Finally
add a fastening for neck.

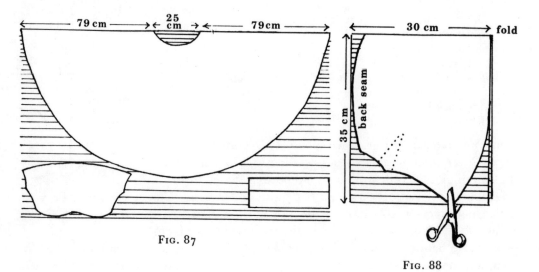

FIG. 87

FIG. 88

PIRATE

You will need:

Striped matelot or jumper
Scarlet scarf for head
Pyjama bottoms (discarded ones)
Wellingtons
2 large curtain rings
Eye-patch
Some black or brown leather-cloth for belt
Card and foil for buckles
Cardboard for cutlass
Make-up for scars, tooth blacking
Material for cummerbund

Cut pyjama bottoms to give ragged appearance. If you are using a jumper wear it back to front. Tie cummerbund round and round and secure with nappy pin.

To make belt. Cut a 2½-inch (6·5-cm.) wide strip of leather-cloth (or use webbing if need be). Cut a large square buckle to fit it, out of strong cardboard, and cover with silver foil. Thread through belt and sew down. This may be strong enough to use as a belt, but if in doubt, add some Velcro to take the extra strain. Cut two smaller buckles, cover with silver foil and attach them to wellington boots with elastic under the foot.

Tie loops of shearing elastic to brass curtain rings so that they may be hung over ears.

Tie scarf round head so that it hangs either at the side or behind.

Paint a proper eye-patch black, buy one from a carnival shop, or make one yourself out of light card.

Cut cutlass out of thick cardboard and spray silver.

Go to town with make-up. Scars, blackened teeth, beard and long hair are all possibilities.

HAWAIIAN GIRL

You will need:

For skirt Natural raffia from a garden supplies shop, and webbing for waist band

For flower garland Crêpe paper in various shades of reds and pinks and very fine wire (floral wire) from the ironmongers. Some thick wool. Pants and bra (if needed), flesh-coloured if possible

(Not an outfit to wear for a winter party)

To make skirt Cut webbing to fit comfortably round the hips with about 1½ inches (4 cm.) over each end. Sew on 1 inch (2·5 cm.) of Velcro. Cut up raffia into lengths you want, and lay down close together in a line the length of the webbing. Dab Copydex on the top ½ inch (1·5 cm.) of each piece of raffia and along webbing. Allow to dry for a few minutes, and then press together.

To make flower garland Cut a 3-inch (7·5-cm.) wide strip off your crêpe paper fold and cut five petals down one side as shown (Fig. 89). Cut off a 12-inch (30-cm.) length. Screw round and round at base to form flower (Fig. 90). Wind a 9-inch

FIG. 89

FIG. 90

(23-cm.) length of wire round bottom of flower, as tightly as possible and secure tail end of wire with the 3 inches (7·5 cm.) of wire that is left trailing. To shape flower, stretch across the centre of each petal with thumb and forefinger of both hands, and separate all the petals, curving them outwards. Make about 2 dozen flowers for garland and two extra to wear behind the ears. Wind stem wires round and round your wool so that flowers are as close together as possible. Cut off all surplus wire.

Wear bracelets on arms and legs. Darken skin with make-up.

SURGEON

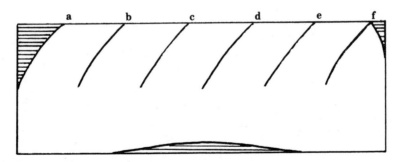

You will need:

> Old white sheet to cut up for overall
> Wellingtons and washable white paint, such as poster
>   paint or distemper
> White lining paper for cap
> Organdie for face mask
> Rubber gloves
> Foil and elastic for reflector (optional)

Make a T-shaped garment with long sleeves and down to the ankles, opening right the way down the back and joining together with three or four pairs of white tapes. Sew on straight upright collar about 2 inches (5 cm.) wide, see Indo-Persian Warrior's undergarment (Fig. 57, page 55).

To make mask see Nurse page 43.

To make cap, measure round head and cut an 8-inch (20·5-cm.) wide strip of lining paper to that length plus ½ inch (1·5 cm.) including curve at base for forehead line. Cut away shaded areas as illustrated in Fig. 91, slitting each of the six sections as marked. Pin together point B to A, C to B, D to C, E to D, F to E and when cap is formed stick together on the inside with Sellotape.

Paint wellingtons.

Cut out disc of cardboard about 3 inches (7·5 cm.) in diameter and cover with silver foil for reflector. Keep round head with some white elastic.

a   b   c   d   e   f

FIG. 91

HAREBELL

You will need:

    Green or cream coloured tights
    2–3 yards (1·8–2·7 m.) lilac coloured net
    Jersey—pale green, lilac or cream
    Green crêpe paper

Measure from waist to knees and cut three lengths of net to that width. Gather each to waist measurement and sew them on to a matching piece of tape. Cut five petal shapes as Fig. 92.

Cut sepals in two layers of crêpe paper for extra strength, and machine round all edges (Fig. 93). Sew on to jersey in one or two places to keep it in place.

To make leaf cap cut five or six leaves out in crêpe paper and stick edges together with P.V.A. glue (see Fig. 94). Glue two leaves at a time and hold in place until they are quite stuck (about 2 mins.). Before joining the ends, ascertain whether the cap fits, and make necessary adjustments before applying glue.

N.B. When cutting crêpe paper make sure that the grain goes vertically down sepals and leaves and the stretch goes across.

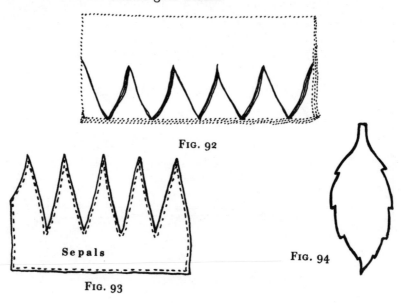

FIG. 92

Sepals

FIG. 93

FIG. 94

ROMAN CITIZEN

You will need:

White material for toga and tunic
Belt
Sandals or boots of white felt

For the first few hundred years after the founding of Rome, men wore the toga without any other garment underneath. With the influence of Greece, the tunic or chiton became a popular additional garment. The tunic therefore can be dispensed with if necessary.

The togas of the senators and magistrates had a border of crimson-purple colour, about 3 inches (7·5 cm.) wide, down the straight edge, and this will add some colour to the outfit, which is otherwise all white.

A toga for an adult is an enormous garment, measuring anything up to 17 feet to 18 feet (5 m. to 5·5 m.) in length, and 10 feet (3 m.) in width. Several joins are necessary even if you are using an old sheet. Obviously a toga for a child is much smaller than this, but to make a well draped and enveloping garment it should measure nearly three times the height of wearer, and should be half that measurement in width. Cut in semicircle as shown (Fig. 95).

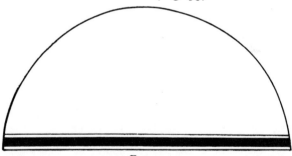

FIG. 95

How to put your toga on: the straight edge is hung from left shoulder down to left foot. The rest of the material is then taken across back, under right arm, allowed to hang loosely round hips, while a length of the straight edge is tucked inside the belt, and the remaining length of fabric is thrown over left arm and shoulder to hang down at the back. Lastly, the straight edge which is tucked in belt and hangs down inside can be pulled out a little to form another fold in the front.

LITTLE BO-PEEP

You will need:

An old rather flimsy dress, preferably with long sleeves
A pair of white tights (worn out)
Edging to suggest lace or broderie Anglaise (you could
    cut up old net curtains)
½ yard (45 cm.) fine cotton for mob cap
4-inch (10-cm.) wide ribbon to tie round and to make
    sash
Black dancing pumps
A long bamboo cane
3-foot (90-cm.) length of thick galvanized wire
A toy lamb

Cut sleeves of dress to make them three-quarter length.
Re-cut neckline to make a deep square. Cut edging and
gather it up to make frills. Cut tights off at ankles and put edging round bottom of
these, as well as round neck and sleeves of dress.

Mob cap   Cut out two circles 18 inches (45 cm.) across. Stitch round edge excepting
3 inches (7·5 cm.) with which to turn it inside out. Sew up gap, then gather up cap
2½ inches (6·5 cm.) round inside edge. Tie circle of ribbon in big bow and sew in
place.

To make crook   Bend wire into shape and stick the two ends firmly down inside top of
cane. Secure in place with electrical tape. If you have time you can papier mâché all
over crook and to make it look like wooden cane, paint it brown. Tie on some
decorative ribbons. Put black pompons on ballet shoes and curl Bo-Peep's hair in
ringlets.

CHINESE MANDARIN

You will need:

To borrow a man's silk dressing-gown
Silk of contrasting colour for cummerbund
Buckram for black skull cap
Black string moustache
Black pigtail attached to cap (buy in carnival shop or
    make with string dyed black)
Slippers (Oriental type)
Make-up for eyes

Dressing-gown should be worn back to front and fastened
tight at neck. Cummerbund should be fairly wide and go
round waist two or three times. For moustache, dip string in black ink and allow to
dry.

To make skull cap　Measure head round largest point and cut to shape with six points
as in Fig. 96, allowing 1 inch (2·5 cm.) each end for overlap. Oversew edges to form
shape (if you wish to make a more luxurious cap, cut a piece of black silk the same
shape, sew it up separately and fit it on top of the buckram cap).

When string moustache is dry stick to a small piece of gauze with Copydex. It
should then be kept on face with the special glue used in stage make-up.

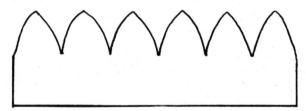

FIG. 96

81

EGYPTIAN LADY

You will need:

Black material for wig (something woolly that looks like
    Persian lamb)
$3\frac{1}{2}$–4 yards (3·2–3·7 m.) of material for sari—preferably
rather flimsy and transparent
Mousse mould (plastic) to make perfumed wax cone
Sandals
Light card for jewellery

To make wig   Cut out the three different pieces as Fig. 97.
Cut patterns in newspaper first to get the size right. Sew
seams together. Paint your plastic mould with some gold
decorations and stick on crown of wig with P.V.A. glue.
    Cut card to shape round neck and arms, and paint on
imitation jewellery to look like turquoise and green enamel set in gold.

To drape sari   Hold material round child's back (waist level) so that corner of one
end is caught underneath right arm (Fig. 98). Take material right round front of
body, round back again, over left shoulder so that the two uppermost corners can
be tied in a knot in the front (Fig. 99).
    Put black eye-liner round eyes to enlarge them.

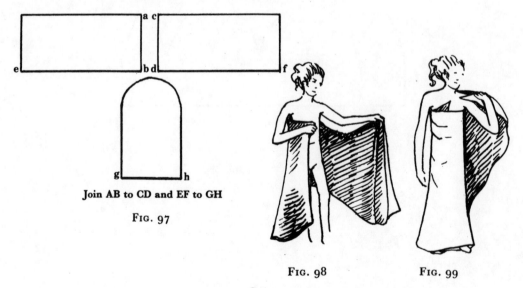

Join AB to CD and EF to GH

FIG. 97

FIG. 98

FIG. 99

ARAB

You will need:

    Striped pyjamas, non-matching top and bottom
    Sheet from a child's cot (must be white)
    Long striped scarf for cummerbund
    Pointed Arab slippers
    Piece of rope or thick cord for headband
    Cardboard for sword

Sew down inside leg seams of pyjama trousers so they fit fairly tightly round calf of leg. Wear pyjama top with collar turned in, unbuttoned and open down the front, and tucked into trouser bottoms.

    Wrap cummerbund round and round waist and secure with a nappy pin.

    Sew rope or cord into a circle that fits snugly round head and cover by wrapping round it a long strip of dark coloured material. This can be made to look even more authentic if you decorate it with some bands of gold paint. Place white sheet on the head of would-be Arab, making sure part of his forehead is covered and then put on top the rope headband which will keep it in place.

    If you have no suitably Arabic shoes cut out shapes in light card and paint as shown (Fig. 100). Fix over slippers with Sellotape. If there is no time for this sandals can be worn.

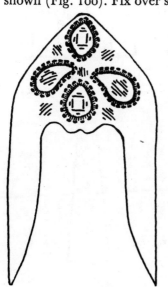

    To make sword that will outlast a party see notes on Crusader's sword, page 53. If you want one just to be used once, cut out curved shape with handle in one piece of stout cardboard, paint all over black and when dry spray lightly with silver paint.

FIG. 100

HAREM GIRL

An outfit for an older sophisticated girl.

You will need:

> Flimsy material for veil and trousers
> Brocade (or something that looks like it) for bodice, belt
>   and apron
> Lots of necklaces
> Sandals (or go barefooted)

Measure child from hips to ankles and allow an inch (2·5 cm.) each end for turnings. Cut trousers to that length and as wide as possible (Fig. 101). Put in elastic round hips and ankles.

From brocade make a simple bodice, which would be improved with a Vilene lining (Fig. 102). Cut out belt so that it is curved over stomach and also long thin apron, which is sewn on separately (Fig. 103). Line both with Vilene.

The veil is a rectangle of material tied at back of head.

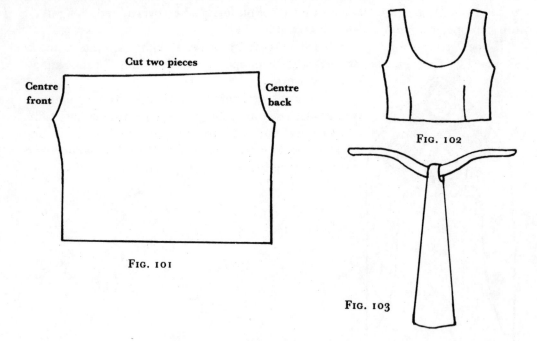

Cut two pieces

Centre front   **Centre back**

FIG. 101

FIG. 102

FIG. 103

JESTER

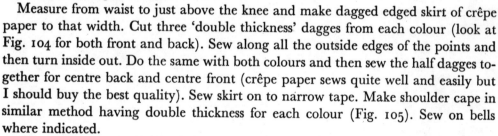

You will need:

> Two contrasting colours of crêpe paper (blue and
>   yellow, red and green, orange and black)
> A pair of white tights
> 2 dyes to match crêpe paper
> A matching jersey
> About 11 bells (from a pet shop)
> A white balloon on the end of a stick (this represents a
>   pig's bladder which was often used in buffoonery)
> Narrow tape for waist-band
> Belt (leather type)
> (*N.B.* 'Dagges' are the edges of material cut in points)

Dye one leg of the tights in one colour first and allow to
dry before dyeing the other.

    Measure from waist to just above the knee and make dagged edged skirt of crêpe
paper to that width. Cut three 'double thickness' dagges from each colour (look at
Fig. 104 for both front and back). Sew along all the outside edges of the points and
then turn inside out. Do the same with both colours and then sew the half dagges together for centre back and centre front (crêpe paper sews quite well and easily but
I should buy the best quality). Sew skirt on to narrow tape. Make shoulder cape in
similar method having double thickness for each colour (Fig. 105). Sew on bells
where indicated.

    P.S. A straighter cut version of this outfit with scallops instead of the dagged edges
and the whole costume in green will turn the wearer into Robin Hood if you complete with bow and arrows.

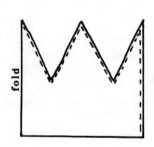
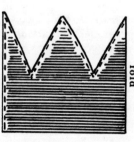
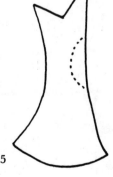
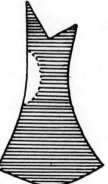

Fig. 104   Fig. 105

MOUSE

You will need:

> Light card for head
> Brown felt for ears and nose
> Brown jumper, tights and stockings

Make a head shaped from the pattern given for the Cat head page 28, cutting it out in light card. Paint it mouse-coloured brown. Cut ears in paper first, to test for size, and then stick felt ears down in place with P.V.A. glue. Do the same with the nose. Stick some bristles from the broom on for whiskers (use Copydex if possible). Draw on round beady eyes and cut small holes in the middle of them to see out.

To make tail sew a long thin sausage out of brown material stockings or felt. Fill with straw or kapok.

Cover hands with stockings.

KING

Clothes for Kings and Queens are not easily produced from everyday clothes. Your best chance may be to acquire some discarded curtains.

You will need:

> Crimson material for cloak
> Patterned material that suggests brocade for gown (or perhaps you already have a dress which will do)
> Gold belt
> Gauntlet gloves
> Lots of cotton-wool for ermine
> Cardboard, gold paint, metallic paper, and a bit of velvet if possible for crown

Measure child from neck to floor. Cut a semicircle with a radius of that length. Cut neckline, and sew on two tapes to fasten cloak together round neck.

Stick a thin border (about 1½ inches (4 cm.) of cotton-wool all the way round sides and hem. Make a large collar that crosses over chest and fastens on left shoulder. Cover with cotton-wool. Paint on ermine marks with black ink. Also put ermine round hem of gown.

To make crown proceed exactly as coronet for Mediaeval Princess, page 47, and then add two crossing pieces of card 14 inches (35·5 cm.) long and 1 inch (2·5 cm.) wide to make the bridge, sticking them together in middle.

Cut 10–12-inch (25·5–30-cm.) circle in velvet (or economize with crêpe paper!) and put inside crown, sticking edges round circumference to keep it in place. Cut out cross and stick on top.

Hair should be long and wavy and parted in the middle.

Wear a moustache and narrow beard.

Put rings on over the gloves.

QUEEN

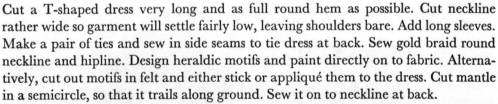

You will need:

> Material for long T-shaped dress which suggests ivory satin
> Old net curtains for mantle dyed gold or possibly rose
> Gold braid for neckline and hipline
> Felt or paint for heraldic motifs in gold, red and blue
> Thin white card for lattice-work earpieces
> Thick card and gold paint for the crown
> Cane for sceptre
> Slippers

Cut a T-shaped dress very long and as full round hem as possible. Cut neckline rather wide so garment will settle fairly low, leaving shoulders bare. Add long sleeves. Make a pair of ties and sew in side seams to tie dress at back. Sew gold braid round neckline and hipline. Design heraldic motifs and paint directly on to fabric. Alternatively, cut out motifs in felt and either stick or appliqué them to the dress. Cut mantle in a semicircle, so that it trails along ground. Sew it on to neckline at back.

To make head-dress. Make your two earpieces in white card with a circle of paper 3–4 inches (7·5–10 cm.) in diameter for each ear, and an encircling strip about 1½ inches (4 cm.) wide. Make crown as for Mediaeval Princess with fewer decorative pieces. Stick cylinders on to sides and cover with foliated bands to link up with crown. Paint gold lattice work on white cylinders (the white represents silk fabric). Stick shiny paper discs to look like rubies and diamonds on crown.

For sceptre cut shape from cardboard, stick on to cane, and spray all over gold.

Make sure hair is all up out of sight.

HARLEQUIN

A fairly elaborate costume for a dancing enthusiast.

You will need:

A long-sleeved white leotard
Thick white tights or narrow cotton trousers
½ yard (45 cm.) pleated white nylon for collar and sleeves
Black belt with silver buckle
Black mask (a fancy one can be bought quite cheaply
from a carnival shop)
Black buckram for tricorne hat
Fabric ink (or poster paint)
Black ballet shoes with pompons or silver buckles
Wood for flap
'Small Latin' moustache

To make the 'diamond' pattern for the harlequin suit most effectively you should print on your pattern with fabric inks (say black, yellow and orange) from lino cuts of 'diamond' and 'narrow strip' shapes (Fig. 106). This way you will be able to wash garments (which may frequently be necessary). If you do not feel up to this, you can paint on the patterns with poster paint. Or stick on coloured paper or fabric. Sew pleated nylon round neck, for collar. Cut tricorne hat in black buckram shaped as in drawing (Fig. 107). Fit head for size and make fabric skull cap to sew in centre. Iron buckram into shape with hot iron, and sew ends together. Make wool pompon and fix in place.

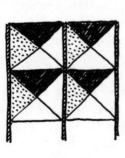

FIG. 106

FIG. 107

FIG. 108

To make a flap See Fig. 108. If you can find time to make one of these you will add a real note of the theatre to your act, for this is the traditional clapper stick that is used in the pantomime. You will need three pieces of wood about 2 inches (5 cm.) wide × ⅛ inch (3 mm.) thick. A short piece in between the two long ones, and the overall length about 18 inches (45 cm.).

COLUMBINE

An eighteenth-century ballet dancer's outfit.

You will need:

Thin silk material and net for dress
A mask
A fan
A chiffon scarf
Doilies to decorate dress
A flower
White socks and ballet shoes

Make dress as for Butterfly, page 29, but with three-quarter length sleeves. The skirt should have plenty of net covered with silk material on top and should be worn ankle length. Colour doilies if necessary, cut out, and stick round them for decoration (if you are making a fairly permanent sort of dress, you should use lace edging). Bodice should be pointed in centre front, and sides of socks should have some decoration.

Hair should be set in ringlets and worn high on head.

A flower in hair or dress, to throw to harlequin, makes a nice finishing touch.

CLOWN

This is the traditional clown.

You will need:

Striped Rugby jersey and matching socks (ideally blue
    and white)
White material for shirt and bloomers
Lace for cuffs
Silk material for ruff (for economy you could use crêpe
    paper)
White buckram for hat
Sausages and carrots to hang out of pockets
Red lipstick and white make-up
Seam binding tape (4 yards approx.)

Cut out very wide garments as shown (Figs. 109 and 110). Sew pockets on to outside
of bloomers so they open through to legs. Paint on large red spots or stick down round
patches of felt. Thread tape through waistband and hem of each leg. Draw up to fit.

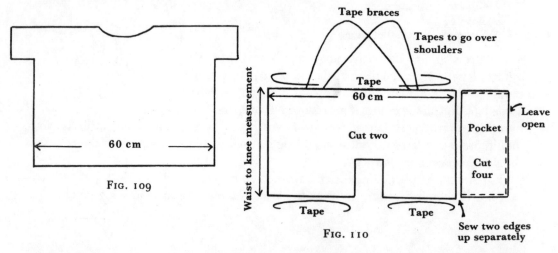

FIG. 109

FIG. 110

To make ruff Measure round neck and add 3–4 inches (7·5–10 cm.). Make a 1-inch
(2·5-cm.) band of that length and iron flat. Cut on the bias two lengths of material
about 5 inches (12·5 cm.) wide and 4½ times the length of the band. Round off the
ends with scissors and fray all edges about ¼ inch (6 mm.). (This is not possible with
crêpe paper!) Then make four ½-inch (1·5-cm.) pleats every inch (2·5 cm.) so that
each ruffle is the same length as the neckband. Place one ruffle on neckband just off-

centre and machine down along the middle of it. Place the other ruffle close beside it and machine down in exactly the same way. This will make the pleats of the ruffle stick out (Fig. 111). Sew on ribbons to tie round neck.

Make conical hat shaped as Fig. 112 making careful measurements of the head. Whiten face and mark on red patches on forehead, cheeks and lips.

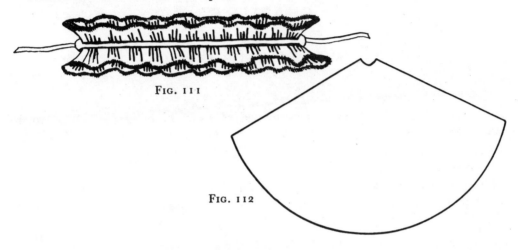

FIG. 111

FIG. 112

A FEW CRAZY IDEAS

MORE CLOWNS' CLOTHES

Borrow a huge pair of grown-up's trousers and make a circle of wire to sew inside round waistband (this will make them stick out all round in the traditional clown fashion). Put long elastic tapes to go over shoulders instead of braces. Shorten legs to reveal brilliantly striped stockings. Wear the largest shoes possible, wearing plimsolls inside if necessary.

Make gigantic spectacles, a tiny bowler hat and a massive bow tie. An ingenious boy could fit the latter up with a light.

A white dickey and collar worn without shirt or over striped T-shirt can also look very funny. If a large jacket is worn over whole ensemble an outsize paper flower should be worn in buttonhole.

If the child likes gags a never-ending silk handkerchief can hang down from top pocket.

CHAPTER 6

Masks and Make-up

From earliest times the mask has been used as a change of identity. It is worth noting that we recognize people by their faces. As long as the head establishes the character, the body is not so important. Perhaps this is why masks fascinate as well as frighten us.

Here are four very simple ways of making them and one rather more difficult. Cut them out in paper or thin card. Bear in mind that all masks are hot to wear, so keep them as light as possible and cut generous holes out for eyes, nose, etc.

1. *Half mask*, Fig. 113 Ideal for birds, and animals, but can be used for people too. Draw in pattern boldly and colour in with felt or fibre tip pens. Nose can be stuck on as a separate piece if you wish, and shearing elastic is used to keep mask on head.

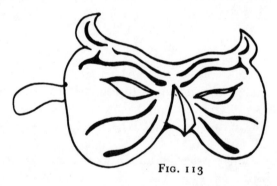

FIG. 113

2. *Whole face mask*, Fig. 114 Draw and colour in face as above. Make a nose from the shape shown in Fig. 115. Cut a hole in mask and stick nose over it. Stick cotton-wool on for hair if you like, and colour it over with poster paint.

3. *Hood mask*, Fig. 116 Slightly more easy to wear. Make the hood out of cotton fabric, sew the mask on to it and blend the colour of both together.

4. *Cylinder mask*, Fig. 117 Cut a length of paper or card and join with Sellotape to form a cylinder. Make a nose as in mask No. 2. Paint on face and make it some paper

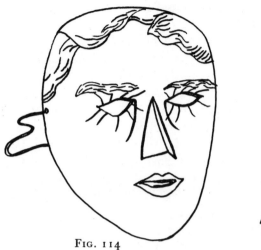

FIG. 114

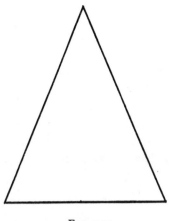

FIG. 115

hair. Cut out very long strips of brown paper about ¼ inch (6 mm.) wide (pointed at one end) and wrap round and round a skewer. Take it off, and run fingernail along it to make a nice ringlet. Make lots and stick all over top.

5. *Modelled head mask*   A much more elaborate thing to make (Fig. 118). This will take a fair quantity of plasticine for the modelling, but do not forget that it can be used again. Choose something with a flat surface to work on. A block of wood for instance. Draw on the board the shape and size of the face to be covered. Cover this area and a little more besides with your plasticine, building it up gradually, bit by bit, until every detail you want is there. Smooth out plasticine on to the board so that it is quite thin round edges. Make sure that nose is raised as high as it should

FIG. 116

FIG. 117

93

be. Next put some P.V.A. glue in a small bowl and thin it down with water. Tear up small pieces of tissue paper, dip them well in the glue and smooth them all over the plasticine face. Apply several layers keeping them as smooth as possible. If you use small pieces you will not have so many creases or air bubbles. When there is an even covering all over face and spreading on to the board, leave everything to dry, preferably overnight. When it has dried rock hard, cut round the edge with a sharp knife and remove from the board. Carefully take out the plasticine from inside, trim the edges neatly round with scissors, and make two small holes at the sides to attach elastic. Paint over finished mask with water-based colours, in any way you like. This mask looks very tricky to do, but as long as you have the time, it is really not too difficult. The end result is very satisfying and when finished is surprisingly strong.

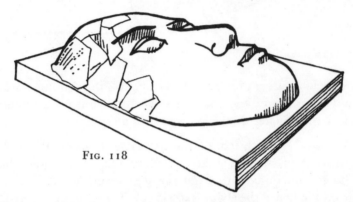

FIG. 118

Make-up This should be kept to a minimum, because it tends to become uncomfortable and hot when children are rushing around. If you do want to put some on for a Red Indian or a Clown for instance, do not forget to smooth cold cream on child's face first. This will enable you to wash it off much more easily. Leichner's are the theatrical make-up people and if you want anything in this line I should certainly buy their products. Joke shops and theatrical carnival shops are wonderful places to hunt for the unusual in the make-up lines. Tooth blacking is a wow! It never fails to cause a sensation, and one bottle will last a lifetime. You can also buy crêpe hair and the special glue to stick it on with, but if you want a cheap, quick moustache, you can always cut one out in card, with two prongs on it to catch it into nostrils. If you do not want to buy ready-made beards you can stick cotton-wool on to millinery wire, and colour it over with poster paint. Large fluttering eyelashes can be effectively made from strips of fringed black tissue paper which have been curled over with a scissor blade. Do you want to make a face look dirty, put veins on hands, or do an Oliver Hardy moustache? Then blacken a cork over a flame and you'll be surprised at the results you can get with it.

And finally, a last hint for would-be sailors. Water-based fibre tip pens are very good for painting on tattoos. Make sure that the colour will wash off by drawing with pen on a piece of paper first and putting it into water. If the colour runs, then it is quite safe to use. Outline your design very boldly in blue or black and then fill in the pattern with red or green. Hearts, dolphins and mermaids are all good nautical motifs.

There are all sorts of ways to make fancy dress as much fun to design and create as it is to wear, and the care and effort you put into making it is well rewarded by the pleasure and excitement it gives.